Good News for All Seasons

Good News for All Seasons

Twenty-six Sermons for Special Days

Richard Allen Bodey, *Editor*

BAKER BOOK HOUSE
Grand Rapids, Michigan 49516

Copyright 1987 by
Baker Book House Company

ISBN: 0-8010-0945-6

Third printing, September 1991

Printed in the United States of America

To
Ruth,
for more than thirty years
Loving Wife,
Resourceful Homemaker,
and
Loyal Partner in Ministry,
whose
Life and Character
are
among the very choicest of sermons

Contents

Preface

A novelist shattered the illusion that writing fiction must be easy because prose is so easy to read. Said he, "You ought to see me some morning when I'm dashing off my stuff—about one inch an hour."

Good preaching, like good fiction—as every preacher knows, but few laity seem to appreciate—is hard work, and preparation is often exasperatingly slow. The chief difficulty, of course, lies in the necessity of facing the same group of people week after week, year after year, and finding something fresh to say that will grip their interest. "If I had to preach to the same congregation Sunday after Sunday, even for a year," confessed John Wesley, "I should preach them and myself to sleep." That from a preacher of rare gifts! What, then, must the preacher of lesser endowments feel when this lion of a task stares him in the face?

The problem is only exacerbated when special days roll round. We all love these festive celebrations with the pageantry and excitement that surround many of them. But pity the poor pastor who has traveled the circuit several times round and whose idea-bag has run empty! For him, familiarity breeds, not contempt, but consternation.

This collection of sermons is intended to help pastors cope with this problem. Editor and contributors alike will feel abundantly repaid if the messages are found to provide seed thoughts that others can cultivate and nurture, each in his own way, as they strive to proclaim the grand certainties of the everlasting gospel in all their luster and power.

We hope that laity, too, will read these sermons, drawing from them fresh supplies of nourishment and strength for their journey of faith.

The collection, it will be noted, is a healthy expression of evangelical ecumenicity. The contributors represent a broad spectrum of ecclesiastical and theological traditions, yet all alike share a common commitment to the historic Christian faith enshrined in the Scriptures and the ancient ecumenical creeds of the church.

Each contributor has been granted freedom to choose the Scripture version of his preference. Unless otherwise noted, Scripture quotations throughout each sermon are taken from the Revised Standard Version.

I must express my deep appreciation to each of the contributors whose generous cooperation lightened the editor's task considerably, and whose unwearying patience in awaiting completion of the project through many long delays has finally been rewarded.

To Allan Fisher, textbook editor at Baker Book House, I am enormously indebted for his wise counsel and welcome encouragement, not least for his enduring forbearance in coaching a neophyte in the ways and customs of the publishing world.

I am grateful to Back to the Bible for permission to use "Let's Examine Our Prayer Life," by Warren W. Wiersbe, and to the Billy Graham Evangelistic Association for permission to use "The Man Who Had It All," by Billy Graham.

Last, though by no means least, I am grateful to my wife, Ruth, who typed—and, because of my mistakes, often retyped—the material for publication.

Richard Allen Bodey
Epiphany 1987

Contributors

Lane G. Adams, Presbyterian Church in America, is senior pastor of Chapelgate Church, Ellicott City, Maryland. Previously associate evangelist with the Billy Graham Evangelistic Association, senior pastor of Second Presbyterian Church, Memphis, Tennessee, and vice president of Biblical Integration for the International Christian Graduate University, Rancho Bernardo, California. Author of *Come Fly with Me* and *How Come It's Taking Me So Long to Get Better?*

David Ralph Barnhart, Association of Free Lutheran Congregations, is pastor of Living Word Church, Eagan, Minnesota, and founder-director of Abiding Word Ministries. Formerly senior pastor of Trinity Lutheran Church (Lutheran Church in America), Minnehaha Falls, Minneapolis, Minnesota.

Richard Allen Bodey, Presbyterian Church in America, is professor of Practical Theology at Trinity Evangelical Divinity School, Deerfield, Illinois, where he is also editor of *Voices*. Previously founding professor and chairman of the Department of Practical Theology at Reformed Theological Seminary, Jackson, Mississippi. Author of *You Can Live Without Fear of Dying* and contributor to *The Encyclopedia of Christianity* and *Zondervan's Pictorial Bible Encyclopedia*.

Richard P. Camp, Jr., Conservative Baptist, is senior chaplain at the United States Military Academy, West Point, New York. Previously dean of students at Gordon-Conwell Theological Seminary, South Hamilton, Massachusetts. After serving as assistant chaplain at West Point for six years, he was appointed senior chaplain by former President Jimmy Carter in 1979.

Paul Arnold Cedar, Conservative Congregational Christian Conference, is senior pastor of Lake Avenue Church, Pasadena, California, and adjunct professor of Evangelism at Fuller Theological Seminary, Pasadena. Previously executive pastor and pastor of Evangelism at

First Presbyterian Church, Hollywood, California. Author of *Why Join the Church? Seven Keys to Maximum Communication, Sharing the Good Life,* and *The Communicator's Commentary: Jude, I & II Peter,* etc.

Charles W. Colson, layman, Southern Baptist Convention, is chairman of the Board of Prison Fellowship International. Previously special counsel to former President Richard M. Nixon. Named Layman of the Year in 1983 by the National Association of Evangelicals. Author of *Born Again, Life Sentence,* and *Loving God.*

Jerome DeJong, Reformed Church in America, is now retired. Previously pastor of Bethany Reformed Church, Grand Rapids, Michigan, and visiting professor of Practical Theology at Trinity Evangelical Divinity School, Deerfield, Illinois. Author of *A Certain Knowledge, God Answers Questions,* and *A Spiritual Pilgrimage.*

Mariano DiGangi, Presbyterian Church in Canada, is professor of Pastoral Studies at Ontario Theological Seminary, Willowdale, Ontario, and executive director of the Bible and Medical Missionary Fellowship. Previously pastor of historic Tenth Presbyterian Church, Philadelphia, Pennsylvania, and president of the Evangelical Fellowship of Canada. Author of expositions on Joel and Jonah, *The Spirit of Christ, Word for All Seasons, I Believe in Mission,* and *Twelve Prophetic Voices.*

Everett L. Fullam, Episcopal Church, is rector of Saint Paul's Church, Darien, Connecticut. Previously professor of Biblical Studies at Barrington College, Barrington, Rhode Island. Author of *Living the Lord's Prayer, Facets of the Faith,* and *Your Body, God's Temple: Seven Studies in Holiness.*

George C. Fuller, Presbyterian Church in America, is president of Westminster Theological Seminary, Philadelphia, Pennsylvania. Previously professor of Practical Theology at Reformed Theological Seminary, Jackson, Mississippi. Author of *Play It My Way.*

William (Billy) Franklin Graham, Southern Baptist Convention, founder of the Billy Graham Evangelistic Association and leader of the weekly Hour of Decision international radio program, has preached the gospel to more millions of people worldwide than anyone else in history. Recipient of scores of awards, he has been named among the "ten most admired men in the world" of the Gallup Poll more often than any other person—twenty-five times in twenty-six years. His picture has appeared on the cover of *Time* magazine. Author of *Peace with God* (more than two million copies sold in thirty-eight languages), *The Secret of Happiness, World Aflame* (on *New York Times* and *Time* magazine bestseller Lists for several weeks), *Angels: God's Secret Agents, How to Be Born*

Again, The Holy Spirit, Till Armageddon, Approaching Hoofbeats: The Four Horsemen of the Apocalypse, etc.

John Guest, Episcopal Church, is rector of Saint Stephen's Church, Sewickley, Pennsylvania, and president of the National Institute of Christian Leadership. A founder of the Coalition for Christian Outreach, a ministry to college students, and a founder of Trinity Episcopal School for Ministry, Ambridge, Pennsylvania. Recording artist of the album *Another Week to Go,* and author of *In Search of Certainty.*

Oswald C. J. Hoffmann, Lutheran Church-Missouri Synod, is speaker on the international Lutheran Hour. Recipient of the Gold Angel Award in 1982, and "International Media Clergyman of the Year," from Religion in Media. Author of *Hurry Home Where You Belong, Life Crucified, God's Joyful People—One in the Spirit, The Lord's Prayer,* etc.

R. Kent Hughes, Independent, is senior pastor of the College Church, Wheaton, Illinois. Previously adjunct professor of Homiletics at Talbot Theological Seminary, La Mirada, California. Author of *Behold the Lamb, Behold the Man,* and the *Christian Wedding Planner* (with Ruth Muzzy).

Dennis Franklin Kinlaw, United Methodist Church, is president of Asbury College, Wilmore, Kentucky, and president of the Francis Asbury Society. Previously professor of Old Testament and Biblical Theology at Asbury Theological Seminary, Wilmore. Author of *Preaching in the Spirit.*

David L. Larsen, Evangelical Covenant Church, is associate professor and chairman of the Department of Practical Theology, Trinity Evangelical Divinity School, Deerfield, Illinois. Previously senior pastor of First Covenant Church, Minneapolis, Minnesota. Author of *In the Saviour's School.*

James Earl Massey, Church of God, is dean of the chapel and institute professor of Religion, Tuskegee Institute, Tuskegee, Alabama. Previously professor of New Testament and Preaching at Anderson Graduate School of Theology, Anderson, Indiana, and campus minister at Anderson College. Author of *The Sermon in Perspective, Designing the Sermon, The Responsible Pulpit, The Hidden Disciplines,* etc.

Kenneth M. Meyer, Evangelical Free Church of America, is president of Trinity Evangelical Divinity School, Deerfield, Illinois, and president of Trinity College. Formerly senior pastor of First Evangelical Free Church, Rockford, Illinois, and executive secretary of the Christian Education Department of the Evangelical Free Church. He has written *Minister's Guide to Financial Planning.*

Joel Nederhood, Christian Reformed Church, is speaker on the international Back to God Hour and speaker-host of the Faith 20 telecast. Editor of *Today* and author of *God Is Too Much*, *The Holy Triangle*, and *Promises, Promises, Promises*.

Theodore M. Olsen, Evangelical Free Church of America, is associate professor of Practical Theology, Trinity Evangelical Divinity School, Deerfield, Illinois. Previously director of Internship and adjunct professor in Homiletics at Trinity, and senior pastor of Arlington Heights Church, Arlington Heights, Illinois.

James I. Packer, Church of England in Canada, is professor of Systematic and Historical Theology, Regent College, Vancouver, British Columbia. Previously principal of Tyndale Hall, Bristol, England, and vice principal of Trinity College, Bristol. Author of *Fundamentalism and the Word of God*, *Evangelism and the Sovereignty of God*, *God Has Spoken*, *Knowing God*, *Beyond the Battle for the Bible*, *I Want to Be a Christian*, *Keep in Step with the Spirit*, *Jacuzzi Religion*, etc., and an editor of the *New Bible Dictionary* and *The Bible Almanac*.

Robert David Preus, Lutheran Church-Missouri Synod, is president of Concordia Theological Seminary, Fort Wayne, Indiana. Previously professor of Systematic Theology, Concordia Theological Seminary, Saint Louis, Missouri. Author of *The Inspiration of Scripture*, *The Theology of Post-Reformation Lutheranism*, and *Getting into the Theology of Concord*.

W. Graham Smith, Presbyterian Church in the United States of America, is senior pastor of Fairlington Church, Alexandria, Virginia. He has served in six different communions of the Presbyterian family of churches: the Church of Scotland, the Presbyterian Church in Ireland, the Presbyterian Church in Canada, the United Presbyterian Church in the United States of America, The Presbyterian Church in the United States, and the Presbyterian Church in the United States of America. In 1949–50, was General Assembly's Evangelist of the Presbyterian Church in Ireland. Several of his sermons have been published in the *Congressional Record*.

Ronald Arthur Ward, Church of England in Canada, died in 1986. Previously canon of Christ Church Cathedral, Frederickton, New Brunswick, examining chaplain to the bishops of Frederickton and Toronto, and rural dean of Saint John. Author of *Royal Sacrament*, *Royal Theology*, *Word Survey of the New Testament*, *The Pattern of Our Salvation*, *Commentary on I & II Thessalonians*, *Commentary on I & II Timothy and Titus*, *The Parables: In the Light of the Cross*, *The Miracles: In the Light of the Cross*, etc.

Warren W. Wiersbe, General Association of Regular Baptists, is general director and Bible teacher of Back to the Bible daily radio broadcast. Previously senior pastor of the Moody Church, Chicago, Illinois, and speaker on "Songs in the Night," an international radio ministry of Moody Church. Author of more than eighty books, including *Walking with the Giants, Listening to the Giants, Be Joyful, Be Real, His Name Is Wonderful, Real Worship, Live Like a King! Bumps Are What You Climb On, Why Us? When Bad Things Happen to God's People, The Wycliffe Handbook of Preachers and Preaching* (with Lloyd M. Perry), etc.

Neil B. Wiseman, Church of the Nazarene, is academic dean at Nazarene Bible College, Colorado Springs, Colorado. Previously professor and chairman of the Religion Department, Trevecca Nazarene College, Nashville, Tennessee, where he also served as chaplain. Author of *Discipleship: Your New Life in Christ, Leadership: A Development Strategy for Church Growth, Rejoice: You're a Minister's Wife, Biblical Preaching for Contemporary Man, Innovative Ideas for Pastors*, etc.

Table of Special Days

The Church Year

Advent Sunday	Sunday nearest November 30
Christmas	December 25
Epiphany	January 6 (commonly observed the following Sunday)
Lent	Begins on Ash Wednesday, the 46th day before Easter
Palm Sunday	Sunday before Easter: the beginning of Holy Week
Maundy Thursday	Thursday in Holy Week
Good Friday	Friday in Holy Week
Easter	The first Sunday after the first full moon on or after March 21: falls between March 22 and April 25
Ascension Day	The 40th day after Easter, which is always a Thursday (commonly observed the following Sunday)
Pentecost	The 50th day after Easter, which is always a Sunday
Trinity Sunday	Sunday after Pentecost
All Saints' Day	November 1 (commonly observed on the nearest Sunday)

Other Special Days

New Year's Sunday	The first Sunday of the new year
Youth Sunday	Commonly observed on the first Sunday of February
World Day of Prayer	The first Friday of Lent
Mother's Day	The second Sunday in May

Father's Day	The third Sunday in June
Independence Sunday	Sunday nearest July 4
Labor Sunday	Sunday nearest Labor Day
Worldwide Communion Sunday	The first Sunday in October
Laity Sunday	The second Sunday in October
Reformation Sunday	The Sunday nearest October 31
Stewardship Sunday	Commonly some Sunday in November
Missions Sunday	Often some Sunday in November
Thanksgiving Day	The fourth Thursday in November (commonly observed on the nearest Sunday)
Thanksgiving Day (Canadian)	The first Monday in October
Bible Sunday	The second Sunday in Advent

Part **1**

The Church Year

1

Come, Lord Jesus
George C. Fuller

> *It was necessary for the copies of the heavenly things to be purified with these rites, but the heavenly things themselves with better sacrifices than these. For Christ has entered, not into a sanctuary made with hands, a copy of the true one, but into heaven itself, now to appear in the presence of God on our behalf. Nor was it to offer himself repeatedly, as the high priest enters the Holy Place yearly with blood not his own; for then he would have had to suffer repeatedly since the foundation of the world. But as it is, he has appeared once for all at the end of the age to put away sin by the sacrifice of himself. And just as it is appointed for men to die once, and after that comes judgment, so Christ, having been offered once to bear the sins of many, will appear a second time, not to deal with sin but to save those who are eagerly waiting for him.*
>
> Hebrews 9:23–28

We are going to begin with a quiz. You can grade yourself. In just a moment I will give you the names of four people who share something in common. You are to guess what it is that they share. If you answer correctly after the first name (not very likely), you get four points; after the second name, three points; and so on. Here they are: Sir Isaac Newton . . . Clara Barton . . . Robert Ripley . . . Jesus.

Their common experience is, of course, that their birthdays all occur on December 25.

If I were to tell you the highlights of the life of Isaac Newton, I would begin with his birth on Christmas Day, 1642, mention his achievements in science and mathematics, perhaps refer to his Christian faith, and indicate that he died in 1727. Clara Barton first appeared on the world scene on Christmas Day, 1821, became known as the "angel of the battlefield" during the Civil War, founded the American Red Cross, and died in 1912. Robert Ripley was born on Christmas Day, 1893, created the cartoon feature "Believe It or Not," and died in 1949. Our sermon text, specifically verse 27, makes clear that for each of these people judgment would come after death. But a complete biography usually begins with a person's birth, summarizes experiences and achievements, and concludes with his or her death.

In the case of Jesus, however, we must say more, much more. Our text does not speak of Jesus' previous existence with the Father, although it seems to assume that fact, so it is proper that we should begin with his appearance here. We also speak of his experiences and his death. But then we must go on to talk about what he is doing now, and, finally, about what he is yet going to do. The biography of Jesus does not end with his death.

What Jesus Has Done

Let's begin at the beginning, on the first Christmas Day. Look at verse 26: "But . . . he has appeared once for all at the end of the age to put away sin by the sacrifice of himself."

The time of Jesus' birth has been fixed at December 25. That guess is based on early tradition, but we have little certainty with regard to its accuracy. The year is thought to be about 5 B.C., although at the time of Jesus' birth, years were counted from the time of the founding of the city of Rome.

The author of Hebrews gives us reliable information about the time of Jesus' coming: it was "at the end of the age." The New English Bible says that Jesus appeared "at the climax of history." All of history until that time looked forward to the great day—the pivotal event of all history—the coming of Jesus. With the coming of Jesus, human experience entered a new phase, a new era, a new age. In the past God had spoken through many prophets and in many ways. Now he speaks through a Son. People of faith had looked for the Messiah, the King, the Lord's Anointed, the Lord of Glory. But their worship had been surrounded by shadows, focused in faith on the future, on hope, on unrealized dreams. In the coming of Jesus, hope is realized, dreams are fulfilled, the shadow becomes substance. The King of Glory has come. A new age has begun. Time has reached its climax. We have moved into the last great age, the time of the preaching of the gospel. The end of the ages is upon us—because Jesus the King has come.

When did Jesus come? In the fullness of time, at the end of the ages, at the climax of history. Now this question: Why did he come?

Jesus came "to put away sin by the sacrifice of himself." It was the Father's plan to redeem his people from their sin, to set them free, to remove sin, its guilt and its power, from them. He purposed to do that through his Son. The name "Jesus" is composed of the Hebrew words for "the Lord" and "save." It is the name "Joshua" in the language Jesus and his family spoke. Of his birth, an angel of the Lord said to Joseph, "You shall call his name Jesus [Joshua], for he will save his people from their sins" (Matt. 1:21). An angel appeared to the shepherds, saying, "To you is born this day in the city of David a Savior, who is Christ the Lord" (Luke 2:11). The story of Zacchaeus's struggle to see Jesus at the Jericho parade comes to this climax: "The Son of man came to seek and to save the lost" (Luke 19:10). Paul said, "Christ Jesus came into the world to save sinners" (1 Tim. 1:15).

The author of Hebrews says that Jesus "has appeared . . . to put away sin by the sacrifice of himself." We have sinned, all of us, from the beginning of time and until this day. God cannot overlook our denial of his sovereignty, his law, and his moral requirement. This is by no means a trivial matter. Blood must be shed, the blood of sacrifice, to nullify sin and to bring its power to nothing. The only question is "Whose blood?" Yours? Mine? The blood of goats and bulls? Jesus came to be that sacrifice, so desperately needed and fully sufficient for every sinner.

Do you clearly understand that this is why he came? Others, like Newton, find their way into careers of science; or, like Clara Barton, into a life of service; or like Ripley, into a life of creative illustration. But Jesus came to die; this was the explicit reason for his coming. Death for him was not an unimportant end to a life of activity. It was the great purpose of his coming. Of him alone is this true. He was born to die. It was not by his teaching that he nullified sin, not by his example, not by his works, however important these all might be. It was by the sacrifice of himself. This is why he appeared: to die.

Did it work? Was it effective? Or did he die, as Albert Schweitzer might have said, a "disillusioned prophet"?

Our text tells us that "he has appeared." Look at that verb. In Greek its tense indicates a past action that has abiding results: "He has appeared." Praise the Lord! He does not need to appear again in humility and endure all over the agony of the cross. His one-time purchase of salvation is effective for all who come to him and claim his sacrifice. "He has appeared." The author of Hebrews elsewhere writes, "We see Jesus, who for a little while was made lower than the angels, crowned with glory and honor because of the suffering of death, so that by the grace of God he might taste death for every one" (Heb. 2:9). His sacrifice was fully effective.

What is hidden here in our text in the tense of the verb is made clear in these words that ring throughout the Book of Hebrews—"once for all." Look at verse 25. The high priest of old had to enter the Most Holy Place every year, year after year without end, making application of the blood of a repeated sequence of sacrificial animals. It is not so with Jesus. He entered the tabernacle of heaven *once for all* on the basis of his fully sufficient sacrifice. He does not need to offer another sacrifice for each sin, each year, for each new generation, ever since the creation of the world. In Hebrews 10:11–12, we read: "Every priest stands daily at his service, offering repeatedly the same sacrifices, which can never take away sins. But when Christ had offered for all time a single sacrifice for sins, he sat down at the right hand of God." His death on the cross is the one and only sacrifice for sins forever.

What Jesus Is Doing Now

All of this is to be seen in that first Christmas, in the first "appearance" of Jesus. His coming occurred at the climax of history. He came for the explicit purpose of giving his life as ransom for many. And his sacrifice is fully sufficient for our deliverance. But Jesus' biography differs from that of Newton and Barton and Ripley. After his appearance here Jesus entered "heaven itself, now to appear in the presence of God on our behalf" (v. 24).

Leviticus, chapter 16, records the commands of God concerning worship on the Day of Atonement. Each year Aaron and the long line of high priests who would succeed him were to follow a carefully prescribed ritual. Once each year they were to take the blood of the sacrificial animals inside the veil of the tabernacle, that is, into the Most Holy Place, where they were to sprinkle it upon the mercy seat and before the mercy seat (Lev. 16:15).

What need was there to sprinkle sacrificial blood on the place of God's mercy? The next verse gives the answer: ". . . because of the uncleannesses of the people of Israel, and because of their transgressions, all their sins" (Lev. 16:16). The blood of the sacrifice had to be applied to God's people. In biblical language that is what "sprinkling" is. "Shedding" blood means, for instance, applying it to the worshiper. But the blood of the victim also had to be applied to the furnishings inside the Most Holy Place. Why? Not because they were in some way sinful, but because sinners were going to dare to enter into fellowship with God. The way must be prepared, made smooth, so that the approaching worshiper would not be consumed as by a raging fire. In this sense, the mercy seat of God in the wilderness tabernacle was "purified." The path was opened, access was made available for a priest, representing the people, to approach a holy and righteous God. But those furnishings in the Most Holy Place and that careful worship procedure were copies of what is in heaven and what is happening there.

Jesus is now appearing in heaven, as the high priest appeared in the Most Holy Place. He is applying the blood of his sacrifice to heaven itself, thereby preparing a place for his people in the presence of the Father. God's wrath does not consume the true worshiper, because Jesus himself has met every demand of this God of justice, who is also a God of infinite love, and whose love sent Jesus in the first place. God can be the justifier of the person who has faith in Jesus, because Jesus appeared to take away sin, once for all. But he can also remain a just God, because the blood of Jesus is applied to heaven itself, making it possible for sinful people to enter the presence of his perfect holiness and blazing righteousness.

Seizing a powerful figure of speech, the author of Hebrews refers to Jesus' work as "sacrifices" (see the end of v. 23). Perhaps he uses the plural noun because he is overwhelmed by the manner in which one perfect sacrifice brings to its conclusion a plan that included centuries of repeated, multiplied sacrifices. All of them are brought to completion in one perfect fulfillment, one offering that is so radical and so dramatic in its effects that the plural is drawn from the author's mind. It is the sacrifice that ends all sacrifices.

That is what Jesus is doing as he now appears in heaven. He is preparing a place for his people. How wonderful it is to know that Jesus is there now, preparing a place. The high priest entered every year, just briefly, only for a few minutes. The next year, the year after that, and every year, he had to repeat the same process, always applying again the blood of imperfect sacrifices to the Most Holy Place of God.

But Jesus does not have to enter year after year, applying the blood of his perfect sacrifice made for sin, once for all, forever (verse 25). His entrance is based on who he is: Jesus, the Son of God, and what he did: he made one sacrifice for sins forever. He entered the presence of God, once for all, on the basis of blood that is his own. Praise God!

May I ask you to underline one little phrase in verse 24? It is the phrase "on our behalf." What Jesus is now doing in heaven is not for his own benefit. It is not for the Father. It is for us, for all readers of the Book of Hebrews who join with its author in faith and obedience to Jesus, God's Son and our Priest before the throne of heaven.

Our text tells us that the specific thing that Jesus is doing for us is preparing heaven for us. Not that heaven needs improving in some way, but Jesus is making it possible for sinful people to come before their holy God. This is not all that his being in the presence of God "for us" suggests, however. He is a "pioneer" (Heb. 12:2), a forerunner, opening a path through the gates of heaven to the worship chambers before the Lord, so that his people throughout all ages can follow. He is doing that "for us" right now.

Jesus is also speaking on our behalf, right now and always (Heb. 7:25). When you do not know what to pray, or how to pray, or do not want to pray at all, Jesus is appearing in the presence of God on your behalf. "If any one does sin, we have an advocate with the Father, Jesus Christ the righteous" (1 John 2:1). We pray so poorly for the right things, or pray for the wrong things, or do not pray at all. "Is it Christ Jesus, who died, who was raised from the dead, who is at the right hand of God, who indeed intercedes for us?" (Rom. 8:34). He is your intercessor, your advocate, your representative, your mediator—Jesus Christ, risen from the dead, now appearing before the Father for his people.

What Jesus Will Do in the Future

So Jesus has appeared once to take away sin. Now he appears once, through these present years, in the temple of heaven on behalf of his people. But our text further indicates that he "will appear a second time, not to deal with sin but to save those who are eagerly waiting for him" (v. 28). He has appeared; he now appears; he will appear again.

It is a general rule that men do not die twice. A man lives, he dies, and after that comes judgment. Men may struggle to deny those two inevitable appointments, but apart from some very unusual divine intervention, they are on everyone's calendar: death and judgment. You don't get a chance to do it all over again. You play the game only once, then it's over, and you await the verdict. There is no "second chance" after death, no correcting of errors, not even space for repentance; the game is over. Only the verdict remains. It is clear in our text and throughout the Book of Hebrews—and, for that matter, throughout the whole Bible—that only those who have identified with Jesus who appeared to do away with sin, only those who have Jesus as their advocate before the Father, only those for whom Jesus himself is preparing a place, can avoid being judged on the basis of their deeds of sin and disobedience, however great or small.

In one sense, Jesus shares the lot of all people. He died only once, in his case "to bear the sins of many." He does not need to die again, not only because this is contrary to human nature (people die only once), but more importantly because he accomplished everything in that death that the Father had sent him to do. As "the Lamb of God, who takes away the sin of the world" (John 1:29), he was sacrificed "once to bear the sins of many." So there is no more death for Jesus, no more dying. What is in his future, then? He "will appear a second time, not to deal with sin but to save those who are eagerly waiting for him." The same Jesus who appeared among the people of Palestine and who was seen to rise to heaven will appear again. Our text is one of the most explicit New Testament references to his "*second* coming." He will come again.

When he appears again, it will not be "to bear sin." The burden of Calvary will be gone, rolled forever from his shoulders. He will not appear a second time "to put away sin." That work is completed. "It is finished," he cried from the cross (John 19:30). On that cross he was the Man of Sorrows, the Suffering Servant. At his second coming, he will be the Royal King who claims his inheritance. He will come to establish for all eternity the complete blessing and benefit of the cross, his first appearing, upon those "who are eagerly waiting for him."

When he comes, he will bring salvation. The victory, already won, will be fully experienced. "Beloved, we are God's children now; it does not yet appear what we shall be, but we know that when he appears we shall be like him, for we shall see him as he is," wrote the apostle John (1 John 3:2). Part of the salvation that Jesus will bring will be the completion of his image in each of his people. We shall be like him.

That full salvation will see the end of Satan's power. Sin will be destroyed. Gone will be temptation; gone will be the struggle. Sickness, sorrow, tears, even death—all will be gone. God "will wipe away every tear from their eyes, and death shall be no more, neither shall there be mourning nor crying nor pain any more, for the former things have passed away" (Rev. 21:4).

These infinite blessings await "those who are eagerly waiting for him," for his appearing. The people of Israel could watch the high priest as he went through the sacrificial ritual outside the tabernacle. But when he entered the Most Holy Place, the priest went alone, and they could only wait and watch. His reappearance would mean that the Lord had looked favorably again upon their sacrifice and that the ritual of the Day of Atonement had been properly and acceptably completed. Those moments when the high priest was removed from their sight were anxious. His return would bring relief and rejoicing. So Jesus' people wait expectantly for his appearance—his coming a second time from the Father's presence. But this time he will appear without any burden of sin and with only the blessings that belong to the King and his people.

Jesus himself told his disciples what it means to wait expectantly for him. In the sermon that he gave on the Mount of Olives just a few days before his crucifixion, he spoke of important future events. He told his disciples that he would return, but that the time of his coming was unknown and would remain unknown (Matt. 24:32–36). How, then, are we to wait properly and live properly while waiting and hoping for that great day?

Jesus commands us, "Watch therefore, for you do not know on what day your Lord is coming. . . . Therefore you also must be ready; for the Son of man is coming at an hour you do not expect" (Matt. 24:42, 44). He tells us to watch and pray (Luke 21:36). He tells us to be busy about his work, being good servants (Matt. 25:14–30). He tells us to minister to the hungry, the thirsty, the stranger (Matt. 25:31–46). "Waiting" is an intensive word meaning "to wait eagerly for." In the Christian context, it calls for thorough personal preparation. It is a longing that demands faith in Jesus, love for him, and ministry to others.

It is not for an end of trials that we long, certainly not primarily. Nor is it an end to sin, to temptation, to suffering, to pain, even to death. Ultimately, we Christians are waiting for *him*, the same Jesus who once appeared to take away sin, who now appears for us before the Father, and who will appear again.

Jesus has appeared to take away sin. Do you have faith that has claimed that act of sacrifice as your own? Are you included among the people of God who claim Jesus as their perfect, once-for-all sacrifice for sin?

Jesus now appears in heaven on behalf of his people. He is preparing a place for us. He is interceding for us. He is our forerunner in the presence of God. Are you aware of what Jesus is doing for you right now? Are you filled with praise and thanksgiving?

Jesus will appear again to bring to final fulfillment all that he has already accomplished. Is that your great hope, your yearning, your expectation, the one anticipation that motivates you to serve him now?

May God give us clear understanding of his Son, who has appeared to take away sin, who now appears in heaven, and who will appear a second time "to bring salvation to those who are eagerly waiting for him."

2

Have You Discovered Christmas?

Richard Allen Bodey

The angel said to them, "Be not afraid; for behold, I bring you good news of a great joy which will come to all the people; for to you is born this day in the city of David a Savior, who is Christ the Lord."

Luke 2:10–11

What could be more familiar to us than Christmas? Ever since we first stared in childhood enchantment at the family Christmas tree with its glistening ornaments and twinkling lights, have we not thought this was the most wonderful day of the year? Have we not listened so often to the age-old story of the baby in the manger, and the angels, and the shepherds, and the wise men following the star, that we can almost recite the sacred lines from memory? Can't we sing many of our favorite carols, stanza after stanza, without even glancing at the hymnbook? Does anyone need to remind us that Christmas is the celebration of Christ's birth?

In spite of that, some of us may not yet have discovered Christmas. Its real meaning may somehow have escaped us. No matter how much we enjoy this season and revel in its festivities, we miss the greatest joy of Christmas until we discover for ourselves its true meaning.

Nowhere is that meaning set forth more clearly than in the angel's message to the shepherds: "Behold, I bring you good news of a great joy which will come to all the people; for to you is born this day in the city of David a Savior, who is Christ the Lord."

What do these words tell us about the meaning of Christmas?

Christmas Is an Event

To begin with, Christmas is an event. The angel announced that a baby had been born that very night in the neighboring village of Bethlehem. The birth of this baby is the most momentous event of all time. Other religions have their myths and legends—some beautiful, some grotesque. But the uniqueness of Christianity is this: the story it tells really happened. It tells us of a divine entrance into our world of space and time, God's own visit in person to our planet earth.

Mind-boggling though it may be, the miracle of Christmas is no mere legend, no parable, no pious myth. From beginning to end, the Christian message is the stirring recital of actual, concrete facts. Its roots lie deep in the soil of human history.

Bethlehem is a place you can locate on a map. You can visit, as I have done, the ancient Church of the Nativity on Manger Square. Parts of this church building date back to the fourth century, making it the oldest Christian church in continuous use. You can even go down into a cavern underneath the church known as the Grotto of the Nativity, which, according to what may well be an authentic tradition, is the very cave where Jesus was born. A silver star in the floor, said to mark the exact place of his birth, bears the Latin inscription, "Here Jesus Christ was born of the Virgin Mary."

True, we cannot be sure of the actual date of Christmas. Most Christians observe Christmas on December 25, although some Eastern Christians celebrate it on January 6. These dates were not fixed, however, until the fourth century, and while neither one is impossible, there is no conclusive evidence to support either of them. In fact, some suggest that Christ may actually have been born sometime in the spring. Moreover, by an amusing quirk of history, even the year of Christ's birth has been miscalculated, yielding the curious result that he was probably born sometime between the fall of 5 B.C. and March of 4 B.C. In any case, uncertainty and error in no way alter the fact that Christmas is a date on the calendar of time. The event it commemorates was as real as the Battle of Gettysburg and Neil Armstrong's walk on the moon.

The Gospels do not point us to some lofty spiritual ideal, dazzling in its charm, captivating in its appeal, but floating forever above our human scene. They confront us with something infinitely more compelling than that. They document the story of a supernatural, yet utterly authentic, earthly career. Saint John sums it all up tersely and simply when he says, "The Word became flesh and dwelt among us" (John 1:14). The one of whom the angel spoke clothed himself with the flesh and blood of our humanity and inscribed his name in the annals of mankind.

When we peel away its layers of sentimental overlay, we find that in many respects the Christmas event was not a very pleasant one. The decree of Caesar, the gossip at Nazareth, the overcrowded inn at Bethlehem, the spiritual apathy of the religious leaders at Jerusalem, and the murderous rage of Herod combine to furnish a dark and somber setting. The Christmas story is a tale of shocking poverty, proud oppression, bitter misunderstanding, malicious rumors, callous indifference, piercing loneliness, heartless rejection, cruel madness. No doubt the baby was cute and cuddly, as most babies are, but how often have you heard of a mother compelled to give birth to her child in a stable and to cradle him in a cattle trough? Was anyone ever born in lower circumstances than Jesus?

The meanness of the manger, however, is transformed into divine splendor, for the infant cradled there is the "Savior, who is Christ the Lord." He is, to quote the majestic words of the Nicene Creed recited in many churches at Christmas, ". . . the only-begotten Son of God, begotten of His Father before all worlds; God of God; Light of Light; Very God of Very God; begotten, not made; being of one substance with the Father." Could any miracle be greater than this, the miracle we call the incarnation? God became man without ceasing to be God. The Creator of all worlds became a creature. The Infinite and Eternal became a child of time.

> Who is He, in yonder stall,
> At whose feet the shepherds fall?
>   'Tis the Lord! O wondrous story!
>   'Tis the Lord! the King of glory!
> At His feet we humbly fall;
> Crown Him, crown Him Lord of all!

True deity and true humanity are now joined in one person forever. That is the paradox of Christmas. The very thought staggers our imagination. Archbishop William Temple put it well when he said that no one has a right to believe in the incarnation at all, who has not first found it incredible. It is all mystery, glorious and sublime. We cannot understand it, and it is futile, indeed downright irreverent, to try to explain it. We are not meant to explain and understand. We are meant simply to believe and to adore.

Christmas Is an Evangel

Christmas is also an evangel, a message of good news. "Be not afraid," the angel said, "for behold, I bring you good news of a great joy . . . for to you is born this day in the city of David a Savior, who is Christ the Lord."

After listening to a Christmas sermon that explained the purpose of Christ's birth in the light of the cross, a man complained, "When I come to church at Christmas, I don't want to hear about the death of Christ. I want to hear something glad and cheerful." His complaint betrayed a widespread misunderstanding of the nature of Christmas joy.

The Christmas message is a mirror in which we confront, bluntly and unmistakably, the truth about ourselves. We are all by nature sinners, rebels-in-arms against God and his government, exiles from his kingdom, strangers to that purity of heart without which no one can see his face and live. There is nothing—absolutely nothing—we can do to save ourselves. We are as helpless before the righteous wrath of heaven as a man trapped behind steel doors in a blazing inferno, sealed off from every avenue of escape.

Christmas is good news because it proclaims that in spite of what we are, God loves us so much that he has provided a remedy for the ruin of our sin. The baby in the manger is not only God come in our flesh; he is also God come in mighty power to redeem us. "Here are words you may trust," exclaimed Saint Paul, "words that merit full acceptance. 'Christ Jesus came into the world to save sinners'" (1 Tim. 1:15, NEB). "The Father has sent his Son as the Savior of the world," declared Saint John (1 John 4:14). Jesus said of himself, "The Son of man came . . . to give his life as a ransom for many" (Matt. 20:28). What are these testimonies—and the New Testament is full of them—but faithful echoes of his name? "You shall call his name Jesus [meaning "Jehovah is salvation"] for he will save his people from their sins" (Matt. 1:21), the angel instructed Joseph. "Crib and Cross," theologian Helmut Thielicke reminds us, "they are both of the same wood." Long ago, Bishop Lancelot Andrewes put it this way: "The scandal of the crib is a good preparative to the scandal of the cross." "Christ was made flesh in the womb of the Virgin Mary," says John Stott, "so that He might be made sin for us on the cross of Calvary."

From the time of Adam's disobedience, God had promised to send the world a deliverer. Throughout the long centuries, the devout in Israel prayed for and awaited his arrival. Now an angel herald broke in upon the stillness of the Judean night to gladden the hearts of humble shepherds with the news that at last the Deliverer had come. In the infant of Bethlehem, God fulfilled his ancient promise to bring salvation to the world. By the sacrifice of himself, this child would overthrow the tyranny of sin and set people free with his redeeming, liberating, life-transforming power.

As you probe your own heart, what would you say you need most to make you happy and at peace with life this Christmas? A new job? A new spouse? A new house? A new car? A bigger income? Better health? A secure retirement? Isn't what you really need most a Savior? Someone who can forgive your sins, cleanse your heart, and put you right with God? Someone who can generate within you new motives, new desires, and new power? Someone who can lift you above the self-defeat, the emptiness, the nagging frustration, and the haunting terror of death that are the common experience of people everywhere? Then Christmas is good news for you. It is the glad evangel of a divine Savior, "the Lamb of God, who takes away the sin of the world" (John 1:29).

> O loving wisdom of our God!
> When all was sin and shame,
> A second Adam to the fight
> And to the rescue came!

Splash it on the headlines everywhere! Let all the earth ring and echo with its joyous sound. "News! Good news! The best news ever! Jesus Christ was born to save!"

Christmas Is an Experience

But Christmas is even more than an event and an evangel. Most wonderful of all, it is also an experience. "To you is born this day in the city of David a Savior." The Christmas Gospel is like a letter addressed to each of us personally. The good news it contains demands our response.

As soon as the angels had vanished into the stillness of the night, the shepherds hurried straight to Bethlehem. There, after diligent search—a touch in the original language lost in our familiar translations—they found a baby, as the angel had said, cradled in a manger. Although Luke does not mention specifically the adoration of the shepherds, artists who have portrayed the scene have captured the spirit of his narrative. Certainly the shepherds could have done no less, for they believed the angel's word and spread abroad the good news about this child to others, praising and glorifying God for all that they had heard and seen.

Is this Savior *your* Savior? Have you welcomed him into your life? Have you by faith claimed the salvation he came to bring? God has given his Son to us. Have you received him? He was born in Bethlehem. Has he been born anew in you? Have you been born anew in him?

Make no mistake about it. Unless he has been born anew in you and you have been born anew in him, he is not your Savior, and you are not saved. You are still in your sins, and being in your sins, you are spiritually dead. Unless this Savior is *your* Savior, you have no hope of heaven, no hope of eternal life, no hope of perfect joy and peace at last in the presence of God. To paraphrase Saint Paul, it is Christ himself living within you who is the guarantee that you will share the glory of God (Col. 1:27). Is your heart his home? Make sure of that this Christmas.

Now and again we read in the newspaper of someone who lived like a pauper, virtually starving himself to death. Yet all the while he had thousands of dollars stashed away at home or deposited in the bank. Could anything be more tragic than that? Yes, it could. A person celebrating Christmas, singing the old, familiar carols, listening to the good news of the Gospel story, yet missing the real gladness of it all because, like the crowded inn at Bethlehem, there is no room in his or her heart for the Savior. That is the greatest tragedy of all.

Do you ask, "How can I be sure this Savior is mine? I know he was born *for* me, but how can I be certain he has been born *in* me?" I ask you a question in return. Are you at all like him? Can others see in you any resemblance to him? Any trace of his character? Any influence of his spirit? Does he make any difference, day by day, in the kind of person you are and the way you live?

Are you, then, more loving than you once were? Are you more patient and tolerant? More courteous and considerate? More appreciative and obliging? More quick to praise and encourage others? More kind and forgiving? More humble and trustful? More earnest and sincere? More thankful and contented? More pleasant and cheerful? More unselfish and generous? More concerned with spiritual interests and more gladly submissive to God's will even in dark and difficult circumstances? More devoted to him and to the service of others in his name?

If Christ has come into your life, you can never be the same person again, for there is one thing Christ cannot do. He cannot enter any human heart without transforming it. "If any one is in Christ, he is a new creation" (2 Cor. 5:17). That new creation always has Christ's image stamped upon it. He comes to live within us to make us like himself.

During the Crimean War, so the story goes, Florence Nightingale passed one night down a hospital ward. As she paused to bend over the bed of a critically wounded soldier, he looked up and said, "You're Christ to me." That is what salvation is all about. We become like Jesus—"little Christs," to use Luther's phrase—so that Christ himself is reflected in us. "We all," says Saint Paul, "with unveiled face, beholding the glory of the Lord, are being changed into his likeness from one degree of glory to another" (2 Cor. 3:18). Increasing Christlikeness is the hallmark of the Christian, the sure sign and seal of the indwelling Savior.

We are all fond of Christmas. It really is the best day of the year. We have been celebrating it merrily every December. But have we discovered Christmas? Have *you* discovered it? There is only one way to do it. We find the secret in the words of one of our most popular Christmas hymns:

> O Holy Child of Bethlehem
> Descend to us, we pray;
> Cast out our sin, and enter in,
> Be born in us today.
> We hear the Christmas angels
> The great glad tidings tell;
> O come to us, abide with us,
> Our Lord Emmanuel.

Will you make this prayer your own? Will you offer it humbly, sincerely, fervently, from the depths of your heart? Then you will discover Christmas. And once you have done that, no one will need to tell you that you have made the greatest discovery of all.

3

Stargazers
Oswald C. J. Hoffmann

> *Now when Jesus was born in Bethlehem of Judaea in the days of Herod the king, behold, there came wise men from the east to Jerusalem, Saying, Where is he that is born King of the Jews? for we have seen his star in the east, and are come to worship him. When Herod the king had heard these things, he was troubled, and all Jerusalem with him. And when he had gathered all the chief priests and scribes of the people together, he demanded of them where Christ should be born. And they said unto him, In Bethlehem of Judaea: for thus it is written by the prophet, And thou Bethlehem, in the land of Juda, art not the least among the princes of Juda: for out of thee shall come a Governor, that shall rule my people Israel. Then Herod, when he had privily called the wise men, inquired of them diligently what time the star appeared. And he sent them to Bethlehem, and said, "Go and search diligently for the young child; and when ye have found him, bring me word again, that I may come and worship him also." When they had heard the king, they departed; and, lo, the star, which they saw in the east, went before them, till it came and stood over where the young child was. When they saw the star, they rejoiced with exceeding great joy.*
>
> *And when they were come into the house, they saw the young child with Mary his mother, and fell down, and worshipped him: and when they had opened their treasures, they presented unto him gifts; gold, and frankincense, and myrrh. And being warned of God in a dream that they should not return to Herod, they departed into their own country another way.*
>
> Matthew 2:1–12 (KJV)

Today we remember the stargazers, those wise men from the east who came to worship the new King born in Bethlehem.

The more you think about them, the more you have to marvel at those men from the east, the matchless Magi. They were seers, not just figuratively, but literally. They observed the stars, and they knew the movements of the stars. They were wise men, learned men, the scientists of their day.

Men of that type might have been expected to pooh-pooh the whole idea of a Messiah sent by God, and even more a Messiah who was born as we are born. Intellectuals often look upon "faith" as the complete surrender of all their intellectual qualities. But who says that faith in God demands the sacrifice and surrender of intelligence? Who says that in order to follow Jesus Christ one must become an unreasoning, unquestioning, gullible, and mindless fool? Wise men and wise women, too, can worship him.

The story of the wise men is told in the second chapter of Matthew: "Now when Jesus was born in Bethlehem of Judaea in the days of Herod the king, behold, there came wise men from the east to Jerusalem, saying, Where is he that is born King of the Jews? for we have seen his star in the east, and are come to worship him" (vv. 1–2, KJV).

I know the story sounds strange, but it is not a legend or a fairy tale. Jesus Christ was born during the days of Herod the king, a real figure in history. Some men who studied the stars came from the east to Jerusalem and asked, "Where is the baby born to be King of the Jews? We saw his star when it came up in the east, and we have come to worship him."

The response of the king, himself a violent and vitriolic man, is completely understandable. It is the way people react when their position is threatened. This man was no fool. King Herod was very upset when he heard about it, and so was everyone else in Jerusalem. He called together all the chief priests and the teachers of the law and asked them, "Where will the Messiah be born?" They answered, "In Bethlehem of Judea." They were thinking of the prophecy in Micah that Bethlehem, though "little to be among the clans of Judah" (Mic. 5:2), would be the one from which would come that leader who would guide his people Israel.

Herod called the visitors from the east to a secret meeting and found out from them the exact time the star had appeared. He sent them to Bethlehem with instructions: "Go and search diligently for the young child; and when ye have found him, bring me word again, that I may come and worship him also" (Matt. 2:6, KJV).

Now that's politics with a vengeance. It is the way politics always gets to be when power is its only goal. It doesn't have to be that way, but that is the way it happens when the object of the game is power—just that and nothing more. Deceit is the name of that game—along with violence, murder, and bloodshed—anything at all, though it might destroy people who get in the way.

So the wise men left. On the way they saw the same star they had seen in the east. When they saw it, they were as happy as they could be, joyfully following it as it went ahead of them until it stood over the place where the child was. They went in and worshiped him.

Just before they returned, they received a message from God, warning them in a dream not to go back to Herod. Wise men that they were, they understood the message. They returned to their country by another road.

I am not here to tell you what kind of a star it was, or how it happened to come up in the east. Others have tried to do that scientifically and have not succeeded too well. Science is a great thing, but it does not answer every question. Great scientists are aware of this, and other people ought to be, too, including theologians.

These wise men from the east did not claim to know everything. But they did know that something wonderful was happening. They followed the star. I wish I knew how they did that. With what they knew, they were able to do it. Their studies paid off. They knew a special star when they saw it, and they were able to follow it.

Why a star? Because a Star had been born in Bethlehem. In a manger there, a little Star from heaven had been born, as babies are born. The New Testament calls him a bright and blazing Morning Star, which heralds the dawn of a new day—God's new day in God's new world.

It is just the dawn of God's new world, but it *is* the dawn. It is a break in the leaden sky, where a star can be seen and followed. Night has departed, and the day is approaching. Let us put off the clothing of darkness and put on the garments of light. It is the beginning of a new day.

The Daystar from on high has visited us, said Saint Peter, a light shining in a dark place, until the day really dawns and the Daystar arises in our hearts (2 Peter 1:19).

The stargazers were looking for a sign of the future. That was their business. The star that appeared in the east brought them back to earth. It led them to the place where the young child was. In that baby, destined for a cross, God has brought hope into the world's darkness.

The coming of that baby marks the promise of a whole new world called heaven. What a world it will be! Where wives won't nag, and husbands will be eternally sensitive and considerate. Children will obey, and parents will listen and understand. Brothers and sisters won't fight, and friends won't stab you in the back. Politicians will always be honest and honorable. Teachers won't be crabby, and students will study. All work will be fun. A world without headaches, upset stomachs, arthritis, cancer, heart attacks, high blood pressure, or the flu. A world without depression, the blues, or the blahs. A world forever free from the scourges of hunger, hate, violence, and war. A world in which people won't become vegetables because of brain damage or advanced senility. A world without tension or fear, where Valium is unknown, and one doesn't have to attempt to escape from unbearable pressures or problems into alcohol and other drugs. A world where love never fades, cools, or grows cold. A world without failure and without disappointment or defeat. A world free of prejudice and bigotry, where the barriers that now separate and divide, causing bitter hostility and suspicion, are gone for good. A world where lambs play with lions, and people can associate with one another without stigma or condemnation. A world where there is no east and west everlastingly warring against each other. A world in which doctors, psychiatrists, and funeral directors will have gone out of business because there won't be any sick or dead people. A world forever free of all the shocks, hurts, wounds, and blows of life that now plague and strike us from cradle to casket. Just think—that star tells us that a new world, prepared by God, has dawned upon us and is on the way to fulfillment.

The true Star is the one the wise men found in Bethlehem. The star in the east, whatever it was, led them to the real Star born in that little cowshed. God's new world is just around the corner because of that little boy, who became that man, crucified and laid in a grave. It is through him, raised from the dead by the glory of his Father (Rom. 6:4), and declared to be the Son of God with power by resurrection from the dead (Rom. 1:4), that the whole new world begins to come into focus.

What we see in that Star of the manger is the One who, as the prophet says, moves the constellations around the way a shepherd leads his flocks. He is in charge. He is doing his own thing, in his own way, at his own good time. You may not believe he is capable of doing that, and you may not trust him to do it, but he *is* in charge. That's what you see, as the wise men saw it, in the place where the young child was, when the star stood still.

These men were very wise and very brave. They were not intimidated by kings. They were impressed by the glory of God. Out of their own great wisdom and at their own peril, they listened to God. Led by the star that they saw in the east, these brave men found the Star of all the stars. They worshiped him with their gifts of gold and frankincense and myrrh, the things they brought with them on their long journey.

Did you ever hear two church members congratulating each other on having come to church through the rain? The martyrs who faced the "lion's gory mane" and the "tyrant's brandished steel" would smile at such a sacrifice—coming to church through the rain. That may be religion, but it takes faith to say,

> Jesus, I my cross have taken,
> All to leave, and follow Thee;
> Destitute, despised, forsaken,
> Thou from hence my all shalt be.

The Magi were men like that, men of faith.

They were persistent. They hung in there until at last they stood in the presence of the King—not Herod, mind you, but the King. When they found him, they knelt down and worshiped him. How else could you approach the King?

All of us could take a leaf out of their book. We are so quick to call it quits, to toss in the towel, to throw in the sponge. After the consultation with Herod, the wise men might very well have turned back. But they did not. They went on, and there was the star. How happy they were, how joyfully they made their way to the place where the child was.

The sight was probably not what they expected. The baby with his poor mother, and Joseph standing by, was not the typical royal scene. But they fell down and worshiped him, bringing out their gifts of gold and frankincense and myrrh and presenting them to him.

The cross on which that King was crucified was not the typical royal scene either. But there it is, in the lordly splendor of kingship, as Jesus the Crucified says to another man also crucified; "Today shalt thou be with me in paradise" (Luke 23:43, KJV).

There it was, on that cross, that he died. Mortal kings die and are forgotten. But he is not forgotten. The world may ignore him, but it will never forget him. He died for the sins of us all, his royalty symbolized only by a crown of thorns. For that he has been crowned with glory and honor, and given a "name which is above every name: That at the name of Jesus every knee should bow, of things in heaven, and things in earth, and things under the earth; And that every tongue should confess that Jesus Christ is Lord . . ." (Phil. 2:9–11, KJV).

When people write "finis" and call it the end, God adds his postscript, "To be continued." The story was quickly continued in the resurrection from the dead. The story is being continued today amid the darkness, the Star shining brightly and pointing to a new world, God's new world, one day to be disclosed in all its glory and splendor.

Don't give up, my friend. There is hope, because there is God. He shows his hand in Jesus Christ. His hand is open to you right now. Christ died for you, and God will forgive you. He forgives all who with contrite spirit and with broken heart confess that they have sinned and ask for his forgiveness. That forgiveness from God in Jesus Christ is the bright star that shines through the darkness.

The wise men loved the Lord and were generous. Consider the gifts they brought, meant for a royal personage. First, there was gold. That's a costly and expensive metal. Is that what God is getting from you, the very best you have to offer of yourself and your treasures, or must he be satisfied with the leftovers, the crumbs, the bones, and the scraps?

The next gift was incense. Incense smells good. In Holy Scripture it is often a symbol for prayer. Is that how your prayers smell to God, like sweet perfume? Or is most of your conversation with God, as well as with everyone else, simply and always crabbing, griping, whining, and complaining? The prayers of God's people, justified by the blood of his Son, come before him with a sweet-smelling savor. He likes to hear your prayers. Pray in anticipation of the day of God's disclosure, his unfolding of his new world.

Finally, there was myrrh. In the ancient world myrrh was used to prepare bodies for burial. If this myrrh was meant for his burial, it was needed for only three days. Some women came to the tomb and the stone had been rolled away. An empty tomb disclosed that he is the Lord of life. He is alive and well. He can be trusted. You can believe in him and be saved by him.

Those brave, persistent, and generous men from the east lead the procession following the Star, which is the Son of God himself. Crucified and risen again, he is the Light that shines upon the whole world today. Let the Light shine into your heart, my friend. The great God who first said, "Let there be light" (Gen. 1:3), shines in your heart this day, "to give the light of the knowledge of . . . [his] glory . . . in the face of Jesus Christ" (2 Cor. 4:6, KJV). He is the Star.

4

Profit and Loss
Everett L. Fullam

We are the true circumcision, who worship God in spirit, and glory in Christ Jesus, and put no confidence in the flesh. Though I myself have reason for confidence in the flesh also. If any other man thinks he has reason for confidence in the flesh, I have more: circumcised on the eighth day, of the people of Israel, of the tribe of Benjamin, a Hebrew born of Hebrews; as to the law a Pharisee, as to zeal a persecutor of the church, as to righteousness under the law blameless. But whatever gain I had, I counted as loss for the sake of Christ. Indeed I count everything as loss because of the surpassing worth of knowing Christ Jesus my Lord. For his sake I have suffered the loss of all things, and count them as refuse, in order that I may gain Christ and be found in him, not having a righteousness of my own, based on law, but that which is through faith in Christ, the righteousness from God that depends on faith.

Philippians 3:3–9

In this third chapter of Paul's Epistle to the Philippians, we find that Paul has made a discovery. He says, "Indeed I count everything as loss because of the surpassing worth of knowing Christ Jesus my Lord." He had learned to count every human effort, every human achievement, as loss, that he might gain Christ. He had come to a point in his life where those things he once thought were so important in order to gain a standing with God, he now considered a total loss. To illustrate that great truth, which Paul wants his readers to understand, he uses the image of a balance sheet, with its assets and liabilities.

Paul tells us that before he came to Christ, there were many things in which he took pride, many things that he felt commended him to

God and that would certainly gain God's acceptance. But, after coming to know Jesus Christ, he says that all of those things he once counted as gain or profit, he now considers to be loss.

We are living in a time in history when almost everybody keeps records. Businessmen keep financial records, as do corporations and housewives, and governments keep records of all kinds. This is also true in the spiritual realm: we keep records for God, and, I might point out, he keeps records on us.

When I say that we keep records for God, I am thinking that so many people often remember the good things they do and set them aside as "Brownie points" to gain favor with Almighty God. Let some difficulty come into their lives, and how often you will hear them say, "Why did this happen to me? After all, I've always lived a decent life." Or, "I belong to church; I'm there all the time; I give my money to it." Their assumption is very clear: they suppose that what they are doing ought to gain God's attention, and he ought to take it into consideration. It is as though they are living in a bargain relationship with him: "I'll do this, and I'll expect you to do your part."

That attitude is universal. It is the human way—doing what comes naturally. Most of us, I suspect, imagine that our standing with God depends upon our being good in some way, or doing good things. We picture our relationship with God as being balanced on some kind of vast celestial scale. On the one side are the good deeds we've done, and on the other side are the evil things. The whole point is to have accrued more good deeds than evil deeds when we die.

That may seem crass, but it is actually the way most of us think of our relationship with God. Because we know how we fluctuate, we have no real confidence in our standing with him. We know how one day we may be up and the next day we may be down. We know how unfaithful we are. If our standing with God depends upon our faithfulness or our accomplishments, no wonder we have no confidence!

But Paul speaks out in a very harsh way about anyone who seeks to add anything to the finished work of Jesus Christ on our behalf. The New Testament teaches that our standing with God depends upon what *God* has done, not upon what *we* do. It teaches very clearly that we do not gain the favor of God by works of righteousness that we have done. The Old Testament prophet Isaiah cried out in the name of the Lord that all our righteousnesses in God's sight are as filthy rags, not to mention our sins (Isa. 64:6). You may be asking how that can be. Is God or the apostle Paul trying to get us to call good things evil? Not at all.

Rather, we are dealing with the pollution effect. When something good passes through a polluted channel, it becomes tainted.

My wife and I spent a month in Zermatt, Switzerland, a few years ago. It is one of the loveliest places on the face of the earth. Zermatt is a village you reach by a cogwheel railroad, and there are no cars there. It is right at the foot of the Matterhorn, and snow-covered mountains tower all around that lovely little village in the valley. But the residents once had a typhoid scare. Some people in the village got typhoid fever, and they tried to hush it up. They didn't want to tell anybody about it. They wondered how any water could be more pure than the water running off the mountains from the melting snows. But they found out that a sewer was located close by the source of the water, and the sewer had bled through and was polluting the water supply. The water was fine as it first ran off the mountains, but by the time it reached the people, it had been polluted.

In a similar fashion, even the good things we do are often shot through with selfish interest, the seeking to advance ourselves in one way or another. So the Scripture says that even our righteousnesses in God's sight are as filthy rags. Jesus said that when we have done our very best, we must still consider ourselves unworthy servants in God's sight (Luke 17:10). It is not possible for us to strike up a bargain whereby we gain God's favor.

Listen to what Paul says about those who would add anything to the sufficiency of the Lord Jesus in this matter: "We are the true circumcision, who worship God in spirit, and glory in Christ Jesus, and put no confidence in the flesh." He is saying that the true circumcision does not consist of those who are concerned with the outward appearance, but rather those who worship God in spirit. The New Testament is very clear about that: "The true worshipers will worship the Father in spirit and truth, for such the Father seeks to worship him" (John 4:23). We are not left in doubt as to what spiritual worship is. Paul says elsewhere, "I appeal to you therefore, brethren, by the mercies of God, to present your bodies as a living sacrifice, holy and acceptable to God, which is your spiritual worship" (Rom. 12:1).

So many times I have said that worship is not just going through the liturgy. Worship is not the singing of hymns. Worship is not listening to the sermon or even coming forward to receive the sacrament. Worship takes place only when there is self-offering, and this, of course, is something that no one can do for us. We can enter into the midst of a worshiping people and be islands of resistance, and God knows this. It becomes possible for us to worship only when we present ourselves as living sacrifices.

Paul says that we are the true circumcision who worship God in spirit and also "glory in Christ Jesus." The more we know of the Christian gospel, the more we come to center our lives in the Lord Jesus. Scripture tells us that it is the will of God the Father for his Son to be exalted to the place of absolute supremacy, and that he has been given a name "which is above every name" (Phil. 2:9). Jesus taught that when the Holy Spirit came, he would not speak about himself; he would glorify Jesus (John 16:14). A Christian is a person who "glories" in the Lord God, who has revealed himself fully and finally in his Son, Jesus Christ.

Paul goes on to say that if one could gain favor with God through any external circumstances, he would have a good head start. He lists some of the things that he would be able to say, if it were possible to gain the favor of God that way. "Though I myself," he says "have reason for confidence in the flesh also. If any other man thinks he has reason for confidence in the flesh, I have more." Then Paul begins to list his reasons for such confidence.

He was "circumcised on the eighth day." In Genesis we read that the Lord told Abraham that his sons and all male children among his descendants were to be circumcised on the eighth day, and that this was to be a perpetual statute for the people of Israel (Gen. 17:9–13). God said that circumcision was to be a sign of their covenant with him. Today we would call circumcision a sacrament, that is, an external sign of something God is doing spiritually. "Any uncircumcised male, " God added, "shall be cut off from his people; he has broken my covenant" (Gen. 17:14).

When Paul says that he was circumcised on the eighth day, he is claiming the authority of a religious rite that was significant because God himself established and commanded it. "Nevertheless," Paul is saying, "I do not place confidence in anything I could have done, even in circumcision, though God ordained it." You see, you can fulfill the will of God externally by doing what he commands, but if you desire to use that obedience as a basis for gaining his favor, then it becomes a hateful thing in God's sight.

Paul continues his argument by noting that he belonged to "the people of Israel." In other words, he was a member of God's chosen race, God's covenant people. More particularly, Paul belonged to the tribe of Benjamin. Of the twelve Hebrew tribes, Benjamin and Judah alone remained faithful to God after the other ten tribes turned their backs on him in disobedience and began to worship in ways contrary to his will. Saul, the first king of Israel, was a Benjaminite. Paul, perhaps, was named for him. So he points out that not only did he belong to the people of Israel, but he belonged to the right denomination! He was, moreover, "a Hebrew born of Hebrews." He was not a late convert, not a God-fearer who attached himself to the worship of the Jews. Not at all! He was *born* a Hebrew.

Next, Paul speaks of decisions he had made. With respect to the law, he was a Pharisee. Although Pharisees do not come off all that well in the New Testament, among all of the Jews of that day, the Pharisees were nonetheless the ones who took their faith most seriously. They believed the Word of God. It is true that they encumbered themselves and everyone else with a hopeless confusion of laws. They turned the whole business of religion inside out and made spiritual worship a matter of fussy little ceremonies, rituals, and rules that had to be obeyed. Jesus spoke very sharply against them. Among all the Jews, however, they were the ones who were looking for the fulfillment of God's ancient promise. They were the believers of the day, and Paul was one of them.

"As to zeal," Paul was a "persecutor of the church." He was so zealous that he attacked all who seemed in any way to threaten what he believed. In another important passage, Paul refers to his fellow-Jews as a zealous people: "Brethren, my heart's desire and prayer to God for them is that they may be saved. I bear them witness that they have a zeal for God, but it is not enlightened" (Rom. 10:1–2).

There are people in our day who think that if a person is sincere enough, that is all that counts. But I remind you that you can be sincerely wrong! You can honestly believe something, but if that belief is not right, it can be disastrous to you, should you act upon it. Sincerity and zeal are not enough. Many Jews in Paul's day had both, but they were unenlightened, he says. And he tells us exactly where their lack of enlightenment lay: "Being ignorant of the righteousness that comes from God and seeking to establish their own, they did not submit to God's righteousness" (Rom. 10:3).

There we have the great question. How shall we come before God? Shall we come bringing all our credentials with us, spreading the record of our good works before the Almighty, seeking his favor toward us because of what we have done for him? Is that how we shall come? If we think so, we need to heed the bad news. God pours contempt on our righteous deeds. They are like filthy rags in his sight and do not measure up.

You may wonder at that harshness. Why? Because you and I, when we measure ourselves with one another, don't look that bad. I could stand alongside some people in my community and look like an absolute paragon of virtue. We can always find people worse than we are. If we measure ourselves by these people, we can congratulate ourselves. But Jesus said, "You . . . must be perfect, as your heavenly Father is perfect" (Matt. 5:48). How do we stand on this scale? I know I don't stand very high!

Perfection is like wholeness. It is all there, or it is not there at all. We can't be half-perfect. To be less than perfect is to be imperfect. And that is the problem. It is not that there is nothing good about us. It is just that our goodness does not add up to the standard God expects of us. What reason does he have to expect so much of us? He is God, and he cannot set a lower standard of behavior than the standard of his own perfection. That is the way God is. He understands, and he has provided a way out, but he cannot lower the standard that he has set for us.

After reciting all his claims and virtues according to the common Jewish religious standards of his day, Paul testifies, "But whatever gain I had, I counted as loss for the sake of Christ. Indeed I count everything as loss because of the surpassing worth of knowing Christ Jesus my Lord. For his sake I have suffered the loss of all things, and count them as refuse, in order that I may gain Christ." You see, before Paul knew the Lord, he thought that being a Jew, being circumcised, being a Pharisee, were all assets, so far as his relationship with God was concerned. But after he came to know the Lord Jesus Christ, all that he had previously thought was his gain, he put down on the loss side of his spiritual balance sheet. One entry alone appears on the gain side—the name Jesus.

Every last one of us—there are no exceptions—is in his own mind standing before God either trusting or not trusting in his own righteousness. There are no other options. In the back of our minds, we are either expecting God to take note of the good things we have done—how much we have given, the church to which we belong, and so on—as the basis for his dealing with us, or else we reject that viewpoint totally out-of-hand. If you plan to appear before Almighty God someday with your list of credentials, I must tell you that in that day God will pour scorn over every bit of it. He will not accept it, nor will he accept any of us upon that basis. This is bad news, but you have to hear the bad news before you are ready to hear the good news.

The good news is that all that needs to be done has already been done. Do you know what the Scripture says? "For our sake he [God] made him [Christ] to be sin who knew no sin, so that in him [Christ] we might become the righteousness of God" (2 Cor. 5:21). That is "The Big Switch." God took all of our sins and placed them on Jesus, and he is prepared to credit all the perfect and infinite righteousness of Jesus to our account the moment we stop trusting our own righteousness and trust Jesus instead. We can't have it both ways. It is not a little bit of Christ and a little bit of me. It is either all of Christ and none of me, or all of me and none of him. There is no other alternative.

The Episcopalian *Book of Common Prayer* contains a beautiful prayer that forms part of the liturgy for the Holy Eucharist. "We do not presume to come to this thy table, O Lord, trusting in our own righteousness, but in thy manifold and great mercies." That is the whole idea: "We do not presume . . ." and yet people do. In the back of our minds, are we counting on something to commend us to God? Our pedigrees? Our accomplishments? The schools we have attended? The good things we have been able to do? Or do we count all these as loss, and even worse than that—as refuse—in order that we may receive the righteousness that is by faith in Jesus Christ alone? Paul says, "I will sacrifice everything to that end."

The word *loss*, which appears three times in this passage, occurs only one other place in the New Testament, in Acts 27. Here Paul describes a shipwreck that he experienced. He says the storm was terrible. The ship was in danger of coming apart and being destroyed. The officers in charge had to decide whether or not to take the cargo that was in the hold and cast it overboard in order to lighten the ship. The cargo was the reason for the voyage. It was wealth to the owner. It was gain and represented profit. But if they held on to it, they would lose everything. They had to get rid of the cargo in order to preserve their own lives. It is exactly the same with us. The cargo of our lives—our strengths and our weaknesses, our joys and our sorrows, our accomplishments and our failures—we must leave them all behind us if Jesus Christ is to be our salvation.

There are several lines of a hymn we almost never sing today, "Rock of Ages," that so beautifully express this truth:

Not the labors of my hands
Can fulfill Thy law's demands;
Could my zeal no respite know,
Could my tears forever flow,
All for sin could not atone;
Thou must save, and Thou alone.

Nothing in my hand I bring;
Simply to Thy cross I cling. . . .

It is very hard to lay down our confidence in the flesh: the things that we have been able to accomplish and acquire, the name we have been able to make for ourselves. Our world has taught us that these are the things that determine our worth, our value, our significance, our identity. May God help us to see that this is a lie. And may he give us the grace to cast aside all confidence in the flesh and to glory in nothing else but the Lord Jesus Christ, in whose grace alone we are able to stand.

5

He Is Coming!
Paul Arnold Cedar

As they approached Jerusalem and came to Bethphage on the Mount of Olives, Jesus sent two disciples, saying to them, "Go to the village ahead of you, and at once you will find a donkey tied there, with her colt by her. Untie them and bring them to me. If anyone says anything to you, tell him that the Lord needs them, and he will send them right away."

This took place to fulfill what was spoken through the prophet:

> *"Say to the Daughter of Zion,*
> *'See, your king comes to you,*
> *gentle and riding on a donkey,*
> *on a colt, the foal of a donkey.' "*

The disciples went and did as Jesus had instructed them. They brought the donkey and the colt, placed their cloaks on them, and Jesus sat on them. A very large crowd spread their cloaks on the road, while others cut branches from the trees and spread them on the road. The crowds that went ahead of him and those that followed shouted,

> *"Hosanna to the Son of David!"*

> *"Blessed is he who comes in the name of the Lord!"*

> *"Hosanna in the highest!"*

When Jesus entered Jerusalem, the whole city was stirred and asked, "Who is this?"

The crowds answered, "This is Jesus, the prophet from Nazareth in Galilee."

Matthew 21:1–11 (NIV)

He is coming!" That was the exciting message that stirred the throngs of people lining Park Avenue in Minneapolis, Minnesota, on a warm, humid July day in the mid-1950s. Dwight David Eisenhower was the president of the United States. On that particular day, he was to ride in a motorcade past my grandparents' home. They were committed Republicans, and Ike was their esteemed hero.

As a young man, it seemed to me we waited an eternity before we heard the excited cry, "He is coming!" As I looked down the avenue, I saw a host of police motorcycles with flashing red lights surrounding a large black limousine. The entourage proceeded quickly toward us. Suddenly it arrived. Sitting in the back of the convertible was the president, waving enthusiastically and sharing generously his famous smile. Then he was gone!

The expectancy and excitement I felt on that July afternoon resembled the experience of many on the day when Jesus mounted the little colt and rode from Bethany down the hill through the Kidron Valley and up the winding road to the eastern gate of the city of Jerusalem. It is that event we celebrate today, nearly two thousand years later. Whenever we celebrate it, we are filled with joy and excitement because we realize that this was no ordinary ride by an insignificant person. It was, indeed, nothing less than the triumphal entry of the King of kings and Lord of lords.

As we explore Matthew's exciting account, we discover that the events of that Palm Sunday and the week that followed were the climactic revelation of the most awesome, eternally significant truths about Jesus.

Jesus Is the King of Kings

First, the crowds were given a glimpse of Jesus as the King of kings. Most of the day's events were the fulfillment of Old Testament prophecies, and all were wrapped in the pageantry of royalty.

Even the colt had prophetic significance. Zechariah's prophecy declared, "See, your king comes to you, righteous and having salvation, gentle and riding on a donkey, on a colt, the foal of a donkey" (Zech. 9:9, NIV). The instructions of Jesus to his disciples were clear. They were to go to the village ahead of them and find a donkey tied there, with her colt beside her. They were to untie them and bring them to Jesus.

How refreshing it is to see that the disciples went out and did as Jesus instructed them. They did not argue; they did not resist; they did what he told them to do. They responded to Jesus as though he was a king. They might have encountered serious consequences. Stealing a donkey in their society was not unlike stealing a horse in the Old West! Nevertheless, they took the risk and obeyed. The disciples had come to love Jesus and trust him. They had forsaken all to follow him. What had kept them going all along was their deep conviction that he was to be the King of Israel—the promised Messiah.

They longed for his kingdom to come to fulfillment. They argued frequently concerning which of them would be the greatest in his kingdom when he overthrew the Romans, corrected the Jewish authorities, and established his dominion. For weeks and months, even years, they had encouraged him to get on with it—to conduct kingdom business, to enthrone himself as the true Messiah and begin his eternal reign.

Now it was happening. Jesus seemed to be ready to fulfill the messianic prophecies! The two disciples returned with the donkey and colt with great haste and excitement. The village and the city of Jerusalem were alive with the news: "He is coming!" "He is coming!" Jesus of Nazareth, the One who had healed the sick, cast out demons, calmed the storms, fed the multitudes, and even brought the dead back to life—this Jesus was coming!

The mood was festive, the spirit was expectant, the response was demonstrative, the acclamations were appropriate only for a king. "Hosanna to the Son of David!" "Blessed is he who comes in the name of the Lord!" "Hosanna in the highest!" These words were shouted by the crowds in fulfillment of Psalm 118:26. They cut branches from the trees and spread them on the road along with their cloaks. They sang, shouted, and cheered. The King was coming! They had, indeed, a glimpse of the King of kings!

Jesus Is the Lord of Lords

Second, the people were given a glimpse of Jesus as the Lord of lords. After having ridden into the city as a triumphant king on Palm Sunday, the next day Jesus surprised the throngs who had hailed him. If we possessed only Matthew's Gospel, we would assume that this part of the mounting drama also occurred on Palm Sunday, whereas Mark explicitly indicates that it happened on Monday (Mark 11:12, 15–17). Instead of establishing his kingdom, Jesus now changed roles. He entered the temple area, where his conduct shocked and upset many who were watching. He drove out all who were buying and selling in the temple. He overturned the tables of the moneychangers and the benches of those who were selling doves.

In the midst of this activity, Jesus quoted from the prophecies of Isaiah and Jeremiah: "It is written . . . 'My house will be called a house of prayer' [Isa. 56:7], but you are making it a 'den of robbers' [Jer. 7:11]" (Matt. 21:13, NIV). He spoke and acted as though he was the Lord. Everyone knew that it was God's temple, but Jesus acted as if it was his own. Not even a king should dare to do that!

Most of the crowd missed the significance of what was taking place. Because they were looking for a king, they missed getting a glimpse of the Lord himself in all his power and majesty and righteous judgment. They missed the significance of the event—that Jesus was calling them to reestablish the temple as a house of prayer, a place to commune with the Lord in spirit and in truth.

As usual, even the religious leaders missed the spiritual significance of things. They were so busy protecting their personal kingdoms and lording it over the people that they did not recognize the Lord when they met him face to face. That is a strong warning to each of us. We are tempted to become so involved in religious activities that we do not have time to see the Lord—to worship and adore him, to commune with him, to be still and know that he is God.

In driving out the moneychangers from the temple, Jesus was acting just like the Lord. His motive was love. He loved those who were misusing the temple and those who were being led astray by them. And he loved his Father and honored the Lord's temple.

He reached out in love to those in need. The blind and the lame came to him for help, and he responded with love. He healed them (Matt. 21:14). The blind were able to see; the lame were able to walk. The Lord brought love and healing and encouragement and wholeness. Jesus was acting like the Lord. He was doing things that only God can do!

The children continued to sing and shout in the temple area, "Hosanna to the Son of David!" (Matt. 21:15). Evidently the adults lost interest. They wanted Jesus to be the King. They wanted the benefits of his potential kingdom immediately—to get the Romans off their backs, to be delivered from oppression and unbearable taxation, to be able to do their own thing in their own way. But, in their minds, Jesus had failed them. He was not acting like a king. They couldn't understand what was taking place. They didn't see him as Lord.

But the children didn't mind. We cannot be sure whether they saw Jesus as Lord through their simple, childlike faith, or whether they simply enjoyed the festivity and didn't want it to end. But of this we can be certain: they continued to honor Jesus.

Dear friends, may it be so with us. Even when we do not fully understand what God is up to, even when we do not like what is going on, let us be faithful in honoring Jesus, in trusting him, even in the dark! Let us hold firmly to the faith that Jesus is the Lord of all light and dark, day and night, principalities and powers, temples and churches, kings and presidents, nations and universes. He is Lord of all—*the Lord of lords*!

Jesus Is the Savior

Third, the people were given a glimpse of Jesus as the Savior. The story of Palm Sunday makes little sense without the cross. The people who wanted Jesus to be the King desperately needed him to be their Savior. An earthly kingdom would not be adequate. At best, it would be temporary. Like all earthly kingdoms, it would come to an end, as had the mighty kingdoms of Babylonia, Syria, Egypt, Greece, and eventually Rome itself.

Jesus would, indeed, rule as King. But first he must fulfill his immediate task—he must be a savior. And not merely a savior, but *the* Savior. Unless and until he became the Savior, all men and women, all young people and children, would be destined for eternal death. But Jesus came to bring life. He did not come into the world to judge or condemn people; he came to give them eternal life (John 3:16–18).

Humanly speaking, his role as Savior seemed so unnecessary. Judas could not understand it, nor could the crowds of people who had hailed Jesus as King. They viewed Jesus as a failure. He had not met their expectations. In our contemporary American terms, he was not "successful." People who fail tend to be an embarrassment, just like football teams that don't win Super Bowls and baseball managers who don't lead their teams to a pennant. Such people become expendable. So it was with Jesus.

Only a few days later, on that dark and dreadful Friday, the crowds now shouted, "Crucify him! Away with him! Save Barabbas, but let's get rid of that imposter who failed us. He masqueraded as a king, but he is a nobody. He's a friend of sinners. He calls himself God. He is a blasphemer, at best; and a con artist, at worst. Crucify him! Crucify him!"

Even his most loyal, committed disciples did not grasp Jesus' role as Savior. He had taught them and explained to them and tried to prepare them, but they did not understand. Seemingly, they did not want to understand. They did not care about "pie in the sky." They wanted a kingdom *now*! They wanted to be "big wheels"—important men who could tell others where to go and what to do. They didn't want to hear about death and suffering and grief and pain. We are just like them. We don't want to hear about such things any more than they did.

Peter, the faithful of the faithful, couldn't stand to "hang in there" with Jesus in his role as Savior. He denied, fled, and wept. Judas betrayed the Savior—sold him for silver, then hanged himself. Most of the remaining disciples scattered. They went into hiding with their fear and grief and even resentment. Jesus had failed them also. He had not fulfilled their expectations. They felt betrayed.

But, thank God, there were the women and John the beloved. They, too, had not fully understood Jesus' role as Savior, and they certainly didn't like the idea. But they were there, at the cross. They witnessed the most awesome event of history—the King of kings and Lord of lords voluntarily becoming the sacrificial Lamb of God, shedding his blood for the forgiveness of the sins of all mankind, offering himself as the Savior of the world, our Redeemer from all sin.

So much irony was manifested in those terrible hours of suffering, pain, and death. The religious leaders missed it all. They did not see Jesus as Savior. They saw him only as a nuisance. They thought they had finally succeeded in getting rid of him—once and for all! They delighted in mocking him: "'He saved others,' they said, 'but he can't save himself! He's the king of Israel! Let him come down now from the cross, and we will believe in him. He trusts in God. Let God rescue him now if he wants him, for he said, "I am the Son of God"'" (Matt. 27:42–43, NIV).

Jesus was dying for them, but they didn't realize it. He was loving them with incomprehensible love, even while they were taunting him with their indescribable hatred. He was becoming their Savior. He was asking his Father to forgive them because they did not know what they were doing. There can be no greater love than that of dying for another—especially an enemy.

That is what it means to be the Savior, and that is what the cross of Christ was all about—the salvation of all who will believe in the Christ of the cross. Jesus Christ chose to be the Savior—to die as our substitute—to pay the penalty of our sins—to set us free from sin and death—to give us eternal life—to invite us to become citizens of his kingdom, which is eternal. The crucifixion of Christ gave the observers a glimpse of Jesus as *the one and only Savior*. And it caused a dying criminal to cry, "Jesus, remember me when you come into your kingdom" (Luke 23:42, NIV).

King, Lord, Savior—Jesus is all of these and more. He is the image of the invisible God. He is the Creator of all things, and all things were created for him. Christ is before all things and is the glue that holds all of creation together. He is the head of the church, which is his body. He has supremacy over all things!

And, my dear friend, he loves you. That is what Palm Sunday is all about. That is what Good Friday is all about. That is what the marvelous celebration of Easter is all about. *Christ loves you*! That is why he came to earth as a baby, lived among us as the personification of love and goodness, died on the cross as the Lamb of God, and conquered death once and for all through his resurrection. The message of the gospel is both simple and profound: all who believe in him will be saved and will have eternal life.

This is my prayer for you, my friend, that you will get a glimpse today of the authentic Jesus, that you will receive him as your personal Savior, will commit yourself to follow him as your Lord, and will become his loyal subject to serve him as your King. Then, on this special day and for all eternity, you will experience the incomparable joy that comes to all who own him as *the Savior of the world, the King of kings, and the Lord of lords*. To him be praise and glory and power and majesty, as he reigns over his kingdom forever and ever!

6

The Master and His Servants
Jerome DeJong

*"You call me "Teacher' and 'Lord,' and rightly so, for that is what I am.
Now that I, your Lord and Teacher, have washed your feet, you also should
wash one another's feet. I have set you an example that you should do as I
have done for you."*

John 13:13–15, (NIV)

Try, if you can, to picture the setting of this narrative. Jesus
and his disciples were in the Upper Room eating the Passover meal
together. The atmosphere must have been tense, because the disciples were fully aware that something was about to happen. They did
not, I am sure, know of the plot that had been hatched against their
Master, but they did sense the antagonism of the leaders of the Jews
against him. They sensed that something sinister was afoot. Jesus had
warned them several times that in Jerusalem he would be delivered up
to the will of the leaders and be crucified, but they did not seem to take
that warning seriously.

While they were reclining, the Bible records, Jesus "got up from the
meal, took off his outer clothing, and wrapped a towel around his
waist" (John 13:4, NIV). All of the disciples must have wondered at this
strange turn of events. Why was Jesus, their Master, doing this? Then,
even more startling, he poured water in a basin and began to wash
their feet. Why didn't the disciples cry out? Why didn't the others, like
Peter, say, "You shall never wash my feet!" (v. 8)? I think they were so
startled that they could not speak. Indeed, I suggest that if Peter had
been first in line, he would have been speechless, too!

59

Even more amazing than the sight of a leader washing the feet of his followers is the fact that this leader is the Lord of Glory. He is the one without whom "nothing was made that has been made" (John 1:3, NIV), and in whom "all things hold together" (Col. 1:17). Surely, this was an astonishing and dramatic presentation of the truth of John 3:16, that "God so loved the world." We have here an excellent passage to ponder on Maundy Thursday, as we think of that night in the Upper Room when Jesus was with his disciples for the last time at Passover.

The Lord and His Servants

"Do you understand what I have done for you?" (v. 12, NIV). The answer was, evidently, "Indeed, we do not." And why not? They did not understand it because it was so totally unexpected. When they entered the Upper Room, there was no servant present to wash their feet. Who had been appointed to this menial task? No doubt the owner of the house or the disciples who made the arrangements had forgotten about it. Of all of those present, who would you think might have done it? The Master of Miracles, the man whom the crowds came willingly to hear? He, surely, would be the last candidate on anyone's list to perform this kind of act. *Yet he did it!*

Isn't it amazing how many times God does precisely what we say he cannot do. In our theological sophistication, we rule out certain deeds as not being worthy of God, deeds he would never do; and he turns around and does them. Many groups today have suggested that miracles and healing no longer occur in our age, that they ceased after the Age of the Apostles. Then God does something so spectacular that we are astonished and need to lay our hand over our mouth and not speak. Jesus, because he was God, acted just like that.

The disciples did not understand fully what Jesus was doing because they really did not know who he was. It is true that they had seen him as a great and powerful worker of miracles and a man mighty in word and deed. When he calmed the storm, they had asked, "What kind of man is this? Even the winds and the waves obey him!" (Matt. 8:27, NIV). Peter had testified, "You are the Christ, the Son of the living God" (Matt. 16:16). Nevertheless, at this point in their spiritual history, they still did not really understand that he was the Lord of heaven and earth. They did not really know that it was to him that every knee at last should bow (Phil. 2:10). Had they fully understood, I think their hearts would have failed them for fear.

Do *we* really understand? Oh, I know we confess that God's Son gave himself for our redemption and paid for our sins. But do the wonder and the marvel of it all really so move us that we can hardly speak? Think on it this Maundy Thursday, so that we do not let the marvel slip away. *This is Jesus: God's own Son!*

I think the disciples failed to understand this act because of their spiritual immaturity. They needed to grow in grace. They were spiritual novices. So often our spiritual immaturity proves a serious block to our full understanding of the deep truths of God.

The Servants and Their Lord

" ' You call me, "Teacher" and "Lord," and rightly so, for that is what I am.' " We must be very clear about this relationship. He is the Lord; we are his servants, or, if you will, his slaves. We call him "Lord," because we are his possession. "For you know that it was not with perishable things such as silver or gold that you were redeemed . . . but with the precious blood of Christ, a lamb without blemish or defect" (1 Peter 1:18–19, NIV). He is the Lord and we are his possession. We belong, body and soul, to him. That's a great and wonderful truth that we must never forget. How can we, like the disciples, argue who is greatest among us—when he is greatest, and we belong to him and thus to one another? The Lord's Supper is a reminder of this sublime truth: his body was broken and his blood poured out for our salvation.

As we become spiritually more mature, we begin to understand these sublime truths more and more. The Holy Spirit has been given to us for the very purpose of teaching us the things of God. Gradually it dawns on our souls that Jesus is Lord.

Furthermore, as Christians we should serve out of a deep sense of gratitude for what Christ has done in our lives. Is our service loving and grateful service, or are we seeking to obtain some favor from God in exchange for it? It is hard to imagine that our service for Christ could be motivated by anything other than gratitude for all he has done for us. We parents want our children to learn to obey us because of their love and devotion to us. Surely, we whom Christ has redeemed cannot do less than serve him as Lord because we are compelled by the inner devotion of our hearts.

The Servants and Their Service

" 'Now that I, your Lord and Teacher, have washed your feet, you also should wash one another's feet. I have set you an example that you should do as I have done for you.' " Some Christian groups take this command literally and actually engage in footwashing. I am not sure that is exactly what Jesus meant us to do. This act, however, does have important implications.

In the relation between Master and servant, self is secondary and obedience first. Our own wills and our own desires must be wholly subservient to the will and purpose of our Lord Jesus Christ. As their Lord, Jesus had every reason to claim the obedience of the disciples and could easily have expected them to wash his feet. Instead, he washed theirs, thus teaching us that all our wishes and desires and plans are subject to his direction.

We can also see here the need for a willingness to do the most menial and unattractive tasks. Many of the saints have served in lowly places because they felt called of God. Think of Mother Teresa in the slums of Calcutta, India. Think of those dedicated Christians who work among lepers. Maybe you and I have tasks we do not really like to do because they seem too lowly or unpleasant. We are saying, "Lord, I am willing to serve you anywhere, but *not* on the midnight shift, or under that supervisor or in that capacity." We are told that David Livingstone prayed that God might send him anywhere, but not to Africa! How often do we fail to serve as we ought because people do not appreciate our talents or never say "Thank you"? By explicitly instructing us to follow his example in washing the disciples' feet, Jesus made plain his call to selfless service. Are you willing to go anywhere and to do anything he asks of you?

To be willing to serve Christ—that is the crucial issue. Watchman Nee asks and answers the question: "To what are we to be consecrated? To the will of God, to be and to do whatever He requires."

Our Daily Bread, published by the Radio Bible Class, tells of a faithful, devoted Christian lady who felt deeply convicted that she ought to do something to show her love for Jesus. The Lord laid on her heart the need of an elderly woman who, though a Christian, was a rather strange individual. Her borderline mental condition caused some to think of her as "an old witch," but this Christian lady knew she was only a poor soul who needed help.

She went to the woman's home and asked if there was anything she could do. The elderly woman needed groceries, so our friend went to the store to buy them. Then, after cleaning and straightening the house, she asked, "Is there anything else you would like me to do?" "Yes," replied the woman, "My relatives usually wash my feet, as I cannot do it myself. Would you do that for me? They have not been washed for months." The Christian lady hesitated, for she was a fastidious person. However, determined to show her love for Christ, she said, "I'll be happy to do so." The task was highly unpleasant and took about twenty minutes of scrubbing, but the poor elderly woman was overjoyed and thankful.

Are you willing to serve like that?

7

God and the Cross
Joel H. Nederhood

And being found in human form he humbled himself and became obedient unto death, even death on a cross.

Philippians 2:8

If you are like I am, you are frequently baffled by the contradictions in life. Those contradictions get you after a while: things that shouldn't be together *are* together. Take an airplane crash, for example, the one that killed seventy-nine people when a 737 crashed into the Potomac after hitting the Fourteenth Street Bridge in Washington, D.C. People on a bridge, sitting in their nice cars shouldn't be decapitated by an airplane, but it happened. The ice gave way beneath the fuselage, and the plane sank like a stone to the river bottom—and that shouldn't be either—a sleek aircraft made for flight becomes the watery tomb of its passengers, all properly strapped to their seats. And the last victim, a baby two months old, with all its life before it, we would say, was pulled from the wreckage days later, dead—a symbol of the overwhelming contradiction that runs through human experience.

In our own lives these contradictions crowd in upon us as we try in vain to beat them away. A mother dying of cancer: only a few months ago she cared for her children and for her husband, lively, loving, and being loved. Now she writhes in pain as the doctors and nurses do all in their power to make her last days bearable. Those who visit her sense the contradiction of it all. It shouldn't be, but it is, and there is nothing anyone can do to change it.

Right within our own selves there are contradictions that mount at certain times of our lives and threaten to take our sanity away. We want so desperately to be the kind of people we know we should be, but we find ourselves falling again and again into traps we seem to have set for ourselves.

The anger and the lust and the jealousy and the need for acceptance that we all have can drive us into strange behavior. Sometimes we can be so ashamed of ourselves. Surely we are better people than our actions often portray. Aren't we? But the contradictions appear once again—the crosscurrents of purpose and desire and conviction—these course through our innermost psyches, and it is the lack of clear, straightforward movement to uplifting goals that destroys us. The lack of unity in our lives, the lack of clarity in our thinking, and the great contradictions that act within us and upon us are shattering.

Contradiction—when two things, two ideas, are brought together that seem not to belong together. This frightens and upsets us. We don't often think about it, but it is this that makes the Christian faith upsetting, too. Yes, when one examines the Christian faith closely, one discovers that at its center there is the most profound and awesome contradiction of all.

At the center of Christianity, two realities are brought together that, according to our way of thinking, should never be brought together. They are these: God and the cross. There, I have said it! It is almost too much to say. I know that we have become accustomed to thinking about this because the Christian church has told the world about it over and over again. There is a season of the year when, for several weeks, attention is riveted on the cross. And so we have actually become accustomed to this greatest of all contradictions.

Or maybe you are one of the "lucky ones" who really don't know very much about Christianity. I don't usually think of those as being fortunate, but this time I think they are. They are able to grasp the full extent of the contradiction that is at the heart of the Christian faith. Really, we all must try to strip our minds clean of all the ideas that have made us accustomed to the cross, and we must see continually anew that the greatest contradiction that ever occurred in the history of the world happened when Jesus Christ was crucified. For when we see that contradiction clearly, our own lives look different. Even more importantly, when we see that contradiction, our faith becomes strong and of high quality. God and the cross: these two realities came together on a knoll just north of Jerusalem, when Jesus Christ was crucified. God and the cross—no, it was even more than that: it was God *on* the cross, the greatest, greatest contradiction.

Surely, the apostle Paul intends for us to see this when in Philippians he describes the preexistent glory of Jesus and the depths of degradation that Jesus experienced when he was executed. He wrote:

> Though he [Christ Jesus] was in the form of God, [he] did not count equality with God a thing to be grasped, but emptied himself, taking the form of a servant, being born in the likeness of men. And being found in human form he humbled himself and became obedient unto death, even death on a cross [Phil. 2:6–8].

Two contradictory realities run right through the words of the apostle. On the one hand, we see the divine glory that Christ Jesus possessed as the only begotten Son of God. Let's look at that.

Jesus Christ is the second person of the divine Trinity, who came into human flesh. When we think of him as the Son of God throughout all eternity, we must think of him in terms of the great throne that God occupies. A throne is the seat of a monarch, and when the Bible describes God, it frequently uses this imagery to enable us to respond to the glory of the Almighty. So Psalm 11 says, "The LORD's throne is in heaven" (v. 4). And Psalm 45 says, "Your divine throne endures for ever and ever" (v. 6).

In the Old Testament, the throne of God is described as exceedingly brilliant and awesome. The prophet Daniel tells of his vision of God's throne:

> . . . thrones were placed and one that was ancient of days took his seat; his raiment was white as snow, and the hair of his head like pure wool; this throne was fiery flames, its wheels were burning fire. A stream of fire issued and came forth from before him; a thousand thousands served him, and ten thousand times ten thousand stood before him . . . [Dan. 7:9–10].

In Daniel's vision, the glory of the individual on the throne is emphasized, and the service of the angels around the throne is highlighted. Here is heavenly magnificence and splendor at its fullest. This is what we must think of when we read in Philippians 2 that Jesus Christ existed in the form of God. The English translation tends to give the impression that the person spoken of here was not really God, for he possessed the "form" of God only. Not so in the original Greek, which leaves no doubt that Jesus Christ was and is God through and through, in essence, totally and absolutely divine.

We all know that it is impossible for us with our earthbound minds and limited imaginations to grasp the smallest element of what God's glory really is. The images from the Bible help us. Perhaps the best we can do is to translate some of the data the Bible provides into images drawn from our own experience. I guess I think of the head of state. There he is with all kinds of services at his disposal. There are people who are ready to wait on his every need. The limousine is always ready whenever he wants to use it. The helicopter is waiting for him anytime he wants it. His jet plane is right there for him. When he makes decisions, he affects many lives. He's in charge. He's sovereign.

Jesus Christ as the Son of God lived in the glorious environment of heaven, receiving the praises of the angels, with all the heavenly hosts waiting to perform his slightest wish. And, with all of this, Jesus Christ as the second person of the Trinity enjoyed the fullness of the divine love that characterized the Godhead. He lived throughout all eternity with the Father and the Holy Spirit. God the Son, who with the Father and the Holy Spirit was and is forever and for all time the one and only true God, is worthy of all our worship and praise, world without end!

All this is true. But also true is this: God the Son became a servant and was executed on the cross. When the hill of execution rang with the sound of hammer blows as the flesh of the Savior was attached to the wooden cross, an event occurred that sends us reeling backward in dismay. "Christ the Mighty Maker died for man, the creature's sin," for the sin of humankind.

Think of what the cross really is. We have succeeded in glorifying it. We have layered it with gold and silver and have fashioned it into a piece of adornment. Today you find the cross lying on velvet in locked display cases in the jewelry store. The clerk will take her key and open the case and lift it out carefully and place it on a gorgeous cloth. She will not walk away while you examine it, for fear you may slip it into your pocket. The cross has become so beautiful. But it wasn't beautiful then.

We must remember that the cross was simply an instrument of execution, and such an instrument is always horrible. Have you ever seen an electric chair? Possibly a picture of one? It is a horrible-looking thing. So was the cross.

The cross had even a special dishonor attached to it, for the Romans used it to execute slaves. Once when they were building a road, their slaves revolted; and the Romans overcame the revolt and then built crosses along the road on which to hang the slaves. They used the cross to show how much they despised the criminals they hung on it.

Not only that: there was a special curse on the cross so far as the Jewish people of Jesus' day were concerned. Later, referring to Christ's cursed death and to a sentence in Jewish law, the apostle Paul wrote: "Christ redeemed us from the curse of the law, having become a curse for us—for it is written, 'Cursed be every one who hangs on a tree'" (Gal. 3:13). For the Jewish people and for the Roman government that carried out Jesus' execution, to hang on public display while one endured all the excruciating suffering of death on a cross was the ultimate in human degradation. There was nothing worse.

But those who know the Bible's message well recognize that there was a curse on Jesus' crucifixion that went far beyond the cruel intention of the Romans, and there was a horror in that death that goes far beyond our natural, horrified reaction to instruments of public death. That extra element was, in fact, so great that what the Romans intended and what we perceive are small compared to it. The fullness of the cross's awesome terror lies in the fact that Jesus, while hanging on that bloodstained wood, endured the wrath of God against the sin of the world.

The apostle Paul writes again: "For our sake he made him to be sin who knew no sin, so that in him we might become the righteousness of God" (2 Cor. 5:21). Now I have taken you beyond human comprehension and brought you to the edge of mystery. It is the mystery of divine love, expressed when the Son of God endured the wrath of God against sin, so that now those who believe in Jesus will not have to experience that wrath of God themselves. They can be saved.

There is an old devotional form, which many Christians use when they prepare themselves to eat of the sacrament of the Lord's Supper, that talks about what we have been discussing. It says:

> Let every one consider by himself his sins and accursedness, that he may abhor himself and humble himself before God, considering that the wrath of God against sin is so great that He, rather than leave it unpunished, has punished it in His beloved Son, Jesus Christ, with the bitter and shameful death of the cross.

The eternal Son of God was crucified. If we have trouble trying to imagine his eternal glory, we also have trouble trying to fathom the depth of his suffering and degradation when he was killed for the sins of his people. At Calvary we are asked to bring together two entities that we can hardly force ourselves to do—but we must—Christ Jesus, the second person of the Trinity, the divine Son of God, brought to the point of deepest shame. There is no criminal in the history of humankind who received a punishment more intense and enormous than his.

That is what the apostle Paul is talking about in Philippians 2, when he reminds us that the person who was crucified was the divine Son of God, who relinquished—let go of—all of his glory so that he could obey his Father in heaven and do the only thing that could possibly save stricken humankind from the curse of sin. This is the great fact at the center of the Christian faith, and it stands before us as the greatest contradiction of all.

If you want to be a Christian, this is what you must believe. A Christian is not simply a person who believes in God. Many people believe in God, but a Christian is a person who believes in *this* God. There are many things we do not know about God, and our curiosity will never be satisfied about him completely. But what we do know about him is magnificent and overwhelming. We know that God in the person of his only begotten Son "emptied himself, taking the form of a servant, being born in the likeness of men. And being found in human form he humbled himself and became obedient unto death, even death on a cross."

If you really believe that God in Jesus Christ has done what we have just been talking about, all of the contradictory events that happen in our world take on a little different color. What are all these contradictions really—the fact that a beautiful mother may be stricken with cancer, that a fine airplane crashes and many people die, that a young boy is run over by a school bus, that you and I are so often mixed up—I ask what are all these, really? Why, they are manifestations of sin.

Sin has entered the universe and the human race because humankind fell into sin—and sin is no joke. Sin is utterly destructive, and it corrupts nature itself as fierce storms and roaring volcanoes cause thousands to die. And it corrupts humanity, where we see it in the meanness that all of us display at one time or another. Sin makes everything much, much less than perfect, and it is sin that makes the great contradictions of our experience more often the rule than the exception. But now we know that God in the person of his beloved Son, Christ Jesus, has come right into the center of the ugly mess that we live in all the time and has experienced for us the ultimate contradiction. At Calvary we see God and the cross brought together; we see God *on* the cross.

Before going any further, I want to tell you, in case you don't know it, that Jesus Christ, who died on the cross, rose again from the dead and is alive right now. But that's another story, and Christians talk about that when they talk about the resurrection. For now though, I just want to show you the way God was willing to humble himself for the salvation of sinful people like us.

So I am asking you to believe what I have just told you about what God did for the salvation of people like us. You can count on it. This is truth: God humbled himself and went to the cross for human sin. Believing this can change everything in a person's life.

It can help us go through some of the things we have to go through as human beings. Our lives are full of contradictory events that tear us apart. I think of a person who is healthy and well one day and paralyzed from the neck down because of an automobile accident the next. It's the same person, one day healthy, the next day devastated; one day with plans and dreams, the next day with nothing to look forward to.

But our suffering looks different when we remember that God has suffered, too. Yes, Jesus Christ, who is in heaven right now, is waiting to hear your prayers when you are in the depths of suffering. He knows what you are going through because he went through it. Somehow your suffering begins to look a little different when you see his suffering and when you remember how much greater his was than yours is. Every sufferer is invited by God himself to compare his or her suffering with Jesus' death on the cross, and in that comparison the sufferer will find relief.

But that benefit is small compared to the greatest benefit of all: when we believe that Jesus Christ is the Son of the living God and that he died on the cross for our sins—when we believe this, our sins are taken away.

Something happened at Calvary that you and I will never know about, for it is something that happened within the mystery of the Divine Being. But that something resulted in Satan's defeat, in payment for sin, and in the establishment of salvation for all who believe. Whatever it was that caused Adam's fall into sin to disfigure creation and bring us all this misery—whatever that was—was made right when Jesus died. There was no other way to accomplish this renewal, no other way to accomplish salvation. God did what was necessary to make absolutely sure that humanity would be restored and that a new creation would be built on the ruins of the old.

You can be a part of this if you believe that Jesus Christ is the Son of God and your Savior. Those who believe this can make it through this life, which is so often painful, frustrating, and even tragic. They can make it through with the joy that comes from knowing that the Son of God who suffered so much on his way to victory will make sure that they will be victorious, too.

8

God's Great Amen
David L. Larsen

I John, who also am your brother, and companion in tribulation, and in the kingdom and patience of Jesus Christ, was in the isle that is called Patmos, for the word of God, and for the testimony of Jesus Christ. I was in the Spirit on the Lord's day, and heard behind me a great voice, as of a trumpet, Saying, I am Alpha and Omega, the first and the last; and, What thou seest, write in a book, and send it unto the seven churches which are in Asia; unto Ephesus, and unto Smyrna, and unto Pergamos, and unto Thyatira, and unto Sardis, and unto Philadelphia, and unto Laodicea. And I turned to see the voice that spake with me. And being turned, I saw seven golden candlesticks; And in the midst of the seven candlesticks one like unto the Son of man, clothed with a garment down to the foot, and girt about the paps with a golden girdle. His head and his hairs were white like wool, as white as snow; and his eyes were as a flame of fire; and his feet like unto fine brass, as if they burned in a furnace; and his voice as the sound of many waters. And he had in his right hand seven stars: and out of his mouth went a sharp twoedged sword: and his countenance was as the sun shineth in his strength. And when I saw him, I fell at his feet as dead. And he laid his right hand upon me, saying unto me, Fear not; I am the first and the last; I am he that liveth, and was dead; and, behold, I am alive for evermore, Amen; and have the keys of hell and of death. Write the things which thou hast seen, and the things which are, and the things which shall be hereafter; The mystery of the seven stars which thou sawest in my right hand, and the seven golden candlesticks. The seven stars are the angels of the seven churches: and the seven candlesticks which thou sawest are the seven churches.

Revelation 1:9–20 (KJV)

John was the first of the apostles to reach the empty tomb. After all, he was the youngest, most agile, most fleet of foot, and far faster than lumbering Peter. John got there first, but he hesitated to enter. He peered into the grave, and then Peter came. One hundred years ago, Horace Bushnell—in one of the great classic sermons of all time, "Unconscious Influence"—first suggested that Peter, characteristically brash in entering the burial place without hesitancy, unconsciously influenced the more timid John to take courage and follow him. The two of them stood surveying the evidence. There were the graveclothes on the ledge of stone. The napkin that had been wound around the head of Jesus lay a short distance away. His body was gone. The tomb was empty.

We read in John 20:8 that John "believed." It was young John the apostle who was the first to believe in the resurrection of Jesus Christ. This son of thunder had been transformed into the apostle of love. This brilliant young man, whom we could later call the Christian Plato, believed in the bodily resurrection of the Lord Jesus Christ. To him it was given by the Holy Spirit to share with us the last words of the New Testament, the Book of the Revelation, in which we are allowed to take some very important soundings as to the resurrection and its continuing power and practicality. This is what I pray we might all sense and feel anew and afresh this day—the resurrection of Jesus Christ and its continuing power and practicality.

Under Pressure

By the end of the first century, the apostle John had become an old man. He still believed. Sixty or seventy years had passed since he stood with Peter inside the empty sepulchre. He still believed in the resurrection! He was the last of the apostles to be alive. Every one of them had already laid down his life as a martyr. Only John survived till then. He still believed in the resurrection! Persecution was raging. Bloodthirsty Domitian, the Roman emperor, had banished aged John to the little island of Patmos, a felons' island, a living tomb twenty-four miles off the coast of Asia Minor, southwest of Ephesus; only twenty-five miles in diameter; a rocky, desolate fastness, a crag jutting up out of the Mediterranean. There was John on Patmos, alone and in exile. And he still believed in the resurrection!

Not everyone believes in the resurrection. Our newspapers indicate that there are men who stand in the pulpits of this city today who speak of the resurrection as a first-century myth. The *Los Angeles Times* not long ago carried an article headed: "Did Jesus Really Rise from the

Dead?" The next caption, startlingly enough, was: "Most Bible
Scholars Say No." We are told that in the nine-seminary theological
consortium in the San Francisco Bay area there is not one major professor in any of these seminaries who still believes in the bodily resurrection of Jesus Christ from the dead. I tell you, dear people, modern
man has lost his ability to identify the truth or recognize a lie. In the
Communist world, "the truth" is what the party says. In the free world,
"the truth" is what the public says, so that today's truth may become
tomorrow's lie and vice versa, and our poor, plunging planet, having
lost sight of any guiding star, drifts from one rocky crisis to another,
scarcely avoiding disaster and destruction.

In a most remarkable and revealing article, the cover story of *Time*
magazine a while back, we are told that modern psychiatry has the
blues. A most astounding article. It asserted that modern psychiatry is
itself on the couch. Psychiatrists are baffled and bewildered because
there is so little empirical evidence that anything they are doing to help
is really making any difference in people's lives. An experiment was
done at Stanford University in which eight apparently normal people
were placed in a psychiatric ward. Although the regular inmates of the
psychiatric ward all realized that the newcomers did not belong—they
were impostors—not one psychiatrist or staff member ever recognized over a period of two weeks that these were normal people. Psychiatry stands stunned, startled, and silent before the problems and
perplexities that are tearing up human hearts and lives. What shall
we do?

There was something that kept John intact as a person, even under
great pressure. Constricted conditions, yet courage and character.
Trouble, yet trust. Loneliness, yet love. Something was keeping John,
the aged exile on Patmos, intact as a person even under acute pressure. It is what I call God's great Amen: God raised up Jesus Christ
bodily from the dead on the third day. John still believed it, and it kept
him intact as a person, even under great pressure.

It was this that kept Martin Luther at the Diet of Worms when all the
pressures were brought to bear upon him to make him compromise
and cave in, to capitulate and crumble. He said, "Here I stand. I can do
no other." It was this that sustained Bishop Ridley and Bishop Latimer
as they burned at the stake in England. It was this that kept John Bun-
yan sane during those twelve years he languished in Bedford Jail. It
was this that kept Mary Slessor going in Calabar in deepest Africa,

through great danger and peril. It was this that kept "Small Woman" Gladys Aylward, that little English serving girl who took the Trans-Siberian railroad across the Soviet Union to China. I had the privilege and joy of meeting her and having her in our church in San Francisco, many years ago. That little woman! We had to get a box for her to stand on so she could be seen behind the pulpit. Gladys Aylward. What kept her under pressure? It was God's great Amen. He raised up Jesus Christ from the dead. And John believed. Do you believe?

In the Presence

This first chapter of Revelation is a glorious passage. John was on the isle of Patmos, "in the Spirit on the Lord's day." There was a dual environment: banished to a rocky recess on the island, but he was in the Spirit on the Lord's day. There in his solitude John heard a voice speaking to him, like the sound of a great trumpet. Poor Voltaire used to complain, "No one speaks to us." Someone spoke to John. It was the voice of a trumpet, a voice that said, "I am the Alpha and the Omega"—the first and the last, the beginning and the end. Alpha is the first letter of the Greek alphabet and Omega is the last letter. This voice that spoke like a trumpet was saying, "I am everything you need. I am everything from A to Z, all that is in between." Every conceivable condition and contingency can be met. Every complex condition and contingency, every combination of conditions and contingencies, can be met because "I am A to Z. I am everything that you need."

When John heard the voice, he turned around and saw seven golden lampstands representing the seven churches of Asia Minor, and walking among the seven golden lampstands was the Son of man. On the island of Patmos, in his loneliness and under pressure, John found himself in the living presence of the Son of man. The impression that experience made upon him is recorded: eight startling aspects of the presence of the Son of man. As we look at these eight aspects that impinged upon the consciousness of John, try like an artist to paint a picture of what is represented here. You will probably have something quite grotesque, because this is a very vividly impressionistic vision. Eight qualities, eight characteristics of the Son of man, struck the mind and heart of the aged apostle. They are a magnificent panoramic view of the Lord Jesus Christ.

First was purity. The Son of man was clothed down to his feet like a priest. John saw him as our great high priest. What a comfort that was. He was clothed in a long robe with a golden sash about him. Centuries before, the prophet Isaiah wrote, "Righteousness shall be the girdle of his loins" (Isa. 11:5, KJV). The very first thing that impressed John in this confrontation with the contemporaneous Christ was purity.

The second thing about the Son of man was eternity. His hair was white as wool, white as the driven snow. Is this to say that the hair of Jesus is white? Not necessarily. This was the vivid impression. He was like the Ancient of Days. There was an eternal dignity about the bearing and appearance of the Lord Jesus Christ. Eternity.

The third thing that impressed John in this confrontation with the contemporaneous Christ was his perceptivity. His eyes were as flames of fire, piercing, penetrating. Nothing was hidden from his eyes. He saw into the very deep, hidden part of the heart. His perceptivity.

The fourth thing that impressed John was his severity. His feet were as burnished brass, brass out of a fire. Brass is a symbol of judgment. He trod upon sin. In judgment he trod out the winepress of his wrath. His severity.

The fifth thing that impressed John was his majesty. His voice was as the sound of many waters as he spoke, like a gigantic waterfall, like a Niagara, like Kakabeka Falls—a great sound, a majestic sound.

The sixth thing that impressed John was his ministry. The Son of man held in his hand seven stars, which we learn from the last verse of the chapter are the seven messengers, the seven pastors of these local churches. They were held in the hand of the Son of man.

The seventh thing that impressed John was the Son of man's weaponry. Out of his mouth proceeded a sharp two-edged sword. The sword is the Word of God—the sword of the Spirit, which is the word of God" (Eph. 6:17, KJV).

The eighth thing that impressed John was the living Christ's beauty. He shone like the sun in its full strength, radiant and irridescent, glittering and glistening.

In this series of symbols and pictures, John seeks to capture and convey and communicate the vivid impression that the Son of man made upon him there in his loneliness and solitude on the island of Patmos. John was unequal to the task, and he fell limp and virtually lifeless at the feet of the living Christ. Here was a light ineffable, a glory indescribable, a beauty incomparable; it was the blinding reality of the presence of the Son of man.

My friend, in your Patmos, in your situation of pressure, there is the

One who would be your Companion, your Friend, your Confidant, your Helper. It is Jesus Christ, who came to the apostle John almost two thousand years ago. He came to John in his purity, his eternity, his perceptivity, his severity, his majesty, his ministry, his weaponry, his beauty, and he so completely overwhelmed the apostle that John fell inert at his feet.

Under pressure, but in the presence—that is such a tremendous thing:

> I want Jesus to be real to me,
> More intimately nigh
> Than e'en the dearest earthly tie.

Christ is alive! He came out of the grave, and he moves into the experience of our lives in all of his multi-faceted perfection and glory and beauty and excellency. On the isle, "in the Spirit on the Lord's day," John confronted the living Christ.

With Power

Picture John, prostrate before the living Christ, unable to articulate further what he sees and senses. Jesus speaks to him. Jesus lays his hand on him. He in whose hand were the seven stars, the messengers of the seven churches, lays his hand on John. Thank God for the touch of his hand upon our lives. Thank God that Jesus Christ still reaches out to touch us when we are down, when we are drained, when we are depleted, when we are desperate. "He laid his right hand on me," John tells us, and he said, "Fear not . . . ." This is the last time in the New Testament that those gracious words are uttered by our Lord Jesus Christ, but how many times he had spoken them to John and his companions in the apostolic band—"Do not be afraid. I am the first and the last. I am the one who is living."

Oh, I love these words: "I am the one who is living. I was dead." The construction of the words "I became dead" is the same construction the apostle used in John 1:14, "The Word became flesh"—"I am the Living One. I became dead, but now I am living forevermore. John, I am alive!"

Can you imagine the impact these words made upon the dear, fragile heart of John the apostle in such an extremity? "I am living forevermore." In the King James Version we have that glorious and gigantic "Amen." Our God is the God of Amen (cf. Isa. 65:16: the "God of truth"). Christ *is* God's Amen (Rev. 3:14). The resurrection is God's great Amen to all that Christ has done. "It is finished!" (John 19:30), Christ cried on the cross and the resurrection was God's *Amen* to that. That Amen means this is sure. This is certain. You can stand on this. Praise God for that! God's great Amen is the resurrection. "John, don't be afraid. I am living forevermore, and you can depend on it; you can count on it."

There is no point in following a loser. There is no percentage in being a disciple of a loser. We need to be with a winner. That is the only way we are going to make it. I could take you today to the tomb of Confucius. That tomb is occupied. I could take you to the tomb of Lao-tze, the father of Taoism. That tomb is occupied. I could take you to the tomb of Gautama, the gentle Buddha. That tomb is occupied. I could take you to the tomb of Mohammed. That tomb is occupied. There are thousands and millions of Muslims in this world who revere and honor that sacred site where the bones of the prophet may be found. I could take you to the tomb of Karl Marx. I could take you to the tomb of V. I. Lenin. Those tombs, too, are occupied.

But, my friends, if we went this day to the tomb where Jesus of Nazareth was interred, that tomb is empty. There is no occupant. His bones do not bleach in the Palestinian sand. God raised him from the dead. "I am alive. I became dead, but I am living forevermore. Amen. And I have the keys." I love that word, the word that Jesus spoke to John in exile, "I have the keys. . . ." "Look, I laid my hand on you and I am holding in my hand the keys of death and of Hades, the unseen realm beyond death. I am holding in my hand the keys." Jesus Christ has the keys to every problem, to every perplexity, to every prison. He has the keys to open the doors that do not yield to us. I thank God that in this universe this morning the keys are in the hands of the living Christ. He is able to cope with every situation. He is competent to satisfy every need. He has the keys in his hand.

One of the leading Marxists and atheists in France not long ago made a bleak and melancholy statement: "We atheists have received no promise. There is no one waiting." How tragic that a human spirit must come to an impasse like this, an immovable obstruction in life, a cul-de-sac, a dead-end street. No one is waiting.

Contrast that with the view of Charles Kingsley, a gifted Anglican preacher, writer, and novelist in England a generation ago. He lay terminally ill in one room, while his wife of many, many years lay in the next room, also terminally ill. She sent in a note to her husband in which she said, "My darling, is it cowardly of me to tremble before the unseen realities of what lies beyond death?" Charles Kingsley wrote back reassuringly, "My darling, it is not cowardly, but we do not need to be afraid. It will not be dark because God is light. We shall not be lonely because Jesus Christ is with us." That is the resurrection and its continuing power and practicality for the Christian. Christ is with us with power to face life and whatever it may hold for us in a strength that exceeds anything that we ourselves possess, in a sufficiency that is far greater than all our resources put together and focused. He is with us. He dwells in us who believe.

A man dreamed that he was walking along a beach with Jesus Christ. If he looked back, he could see along that beach two sets of footprints. Jesus had walked with him. But as he looked more closely at the route he had walked with Jesus, he saw that there were stretches of the beach on which there was but one set of footprints. He recognized that those stretches where there was but one set of footprints were the darkest and the most difficult and the most trying times of his life. His most depressing and distressing hours were the hours when there was only one set of footprints in the sand. He turned to Jesus and said, "Savior, I thought you promised that you would be with me. I thought you promised that you would never desert me or forsake me or fail me. I thought, Jesus, that you promised that when I needed you, you would be there. But when I look back I can see that in the darkest and most difficult hours of my life there is only one set of footprints." And Jesus said to him, "My dear child, I promised you that I would not leave you or forsake you. I promised you I would be there when you needed me. Don't you understand that where there is but one set of footprints, I picked you up and carried you in my arms?"

Dear people, Jesus lives. He was dead, but he lives forevermore. And it is his presence and his power that supply us just what we need most.

> I need Jesus,
> My need I now confess;
> No Friend like Him
> In times of deep distress.

He lays his hand on us. He picks us up and carries us in his strong arms. The Son of man. Do you know him? Do you love him? Are you walking with him? He wants to be your Savior and your Lord.

9

The Ascension
Ronald Arthur Ward

> *When he had spoken these things, while they beheld, he was taken up; and a cloud received him out of their sight. And while they looked stedfastly toward heaven as he went up, behold, two men stood by them in white apparel; Which also said, Ye men of Galilee, why stand ye gazing up into heaven? this same Jesus, which is taken up from you into heaven, shall so come in like manner as ye have seen him go into heaven.*
>
> Acts 1:9–11 (KJV)

Some people reason that the first venture into space was a dismal failure. The astronaut took off. All seemed well. Up he went but he never entered orbit. Instead he continued in a direct line towards the remotest regions of outer space. He has been doing it for nearly two thousand years. How far away he is now!

Such is the mockery of the blasphemer.

It leaves us with a question. What *is* "the ascension"? It may be viewed from three standpoints: the human standpoint, the angelic standpoint, and the divine standpoint.

From the human standpoint, the Lord arose in majesty, and the disciples saw him travel into heaven. "Heaven" here must mean the sky. The cloud that "received him out of their sight" must have been a low cloud. Otherwise how could they have seen him disappear into it? If the cloud ceiling had been high, the Lord would have appeared like a distant grain of sand long before he reached the cloud—a speck in the sky. The cloud was very low, probably no higher than the length of a ladder, as in Jacob's dream (Gen. 28:12).

From the angelic standpoint, the Lord returned to heaven. This is where God is (Matt. 6:9–10, 20), and where the angels are (Matt. 18:10; 22:30). It is God's throne (Matt. 23:22; Acts 7:49). From here divine wrath is revealed (Rom. 1:18). The references to sky and heaven are used together in Matthew 6:26. The birds of heaven are in the *sky* ("the air"). Your heavenly Father is in *heaven*.

From the divine standpoint, what God sees in the ascension is one of the richest concepts in the New Testament.

God sees *accomplishment*. The Lord's work is finished (John 19:28, 30). It is because of the cross that he was exalted. He was obedient to the extent of death, death on a cross. Therefore, God super-exalted him and gave him the name that is above every name, the name of Lord (Phil. 2:8–9). He is now ready to give the Holy Spirit (John 16:7). The Holy Spirit does not replace Jesus but brings him. He is a new mode of the presence of Jesus, God's method of providing the presence of Jesus.

God also sees *permanence*. Jesus is seated at the right hand of God. The ancient priest stood day after day at his liturgical drudgery, time after time offering sacrifices that accomplished nothing (Heb. 10:11–12). But Jesus is seated permanently. We ourselves show a contrast to this "permanence" in our ordinary lives. We pay a hurried call and enter our friend's house. "No, thanks, I won't sit down. I can't stay. I'm in a fearful hurry. I just wanted you to know that. . . ."

Although, in the New Testament, our Lord is generally described as being seated, there are exceptions. When Stephen was being persecuted, he saw the heavens gaping wide and the Son of man standing on the right hand of God (Acts 7:55–56). The ascended Lord eagerly arose to help his stricken servant, to welcome him to heaven, and to confess him before the Father, in accordance with his earlier promise: "Whosoever . . . shall confess me before men, him will I confess also before my Father which is in heaven" (Matt. 10:32, KJV). The Lamb in heaven is likewise standing, ever welcoming his own (Rev. 5:6).

God also sees *authority*. The ascended Lord has the right to act. We know the scene. "He is my right-hand man," a businessman says of an enterprising worker. "I sit back and watch him run the business."

I was once taken up the west coast of British Columbia to visit logging camps. As we were approaching Vancouver on our return, the captain asked me to take the wheel. I kept the ship on course, and the captain stood beside me. As befits one who has authority, Jesus is enthroned. He has a throne, and the Father has a throne (Rev. 3:21), but

the throne is one: "the throne of God and of the Lamb" (Rev. 22:3).
That's it exactly! As in the case of the ship approaching Vancouver, the
Son is at the helm and the Father is at his side.

Further, God sees his Son *waiting*. After offering his one sacrifice for
sins, the Son took his seat forever on the right hand of God, *from then on*
waiting until his enemies should be made the footstool of his feet (Heb.
10:12–13). The second Joshua will openly do to his enemies what the
first Joshua had commanded in his time: "put your feet upon the necks
of these kings" (Josh. 10:24).

What does the Son do while he is "waiting"? God sees him *interceding*. The whole world is answerable to God but has no answer. Jesus
gave the answer on the cross. He took the judgment that should have
fallen upon us. We are responsible but have nothing to say. He assumed responsibility for us.

Therefore, in heaven he speaks for us. If anyone sins, we have an
Advocate with the Father—a Counselor, a defending Attorney—Jesus
Christ the just. And he is the propitiation for our sins (1 John 2:1–2). It is
sometimes assumed that here love pleads with justice: the loving Jesus
pleads with the just God. But it is exactly the reverse: justice pleads
with love. Jesus is just and God is love (1 John 4:8, 16).

Imagine the scene. A believer sins. Jesus looks to the Father and
speaks to him: "Father, do not punish this man. I have already taken all
his punishment. I take full responsibility for him." The Father replies,
"Just so, my Son; that is precisely what I sent you to do."

Then, too, God sees *power and sovereignty*. As we have already observed, Jesus has authority, the right to act. Now we notice that he also
has the *ability* to act. Some have authority, like a duly appointed general
whose army has fled. Others have the ability to act, like insurgent
forces; but they have no authority. Jesus has both authority and power.

What does the Son do with his power? He controls the universe, the
whole setup in time and space, and he keeps it in being. All things co-
here in him (Col. 1:17). It is through him that the universe is a system, a
unity in which every part is related to every other part and to the whole
of which it is a part.

If the Lord is the Master of the universe, nothing in the universe can
prevent the preaching of the gospel. Fog may prevent the punctual arrival of the preacher's airplane. A landslide may block his train. A
storm at sea may delay his ship. A breakdown of power may put the
high-voltage cables out of action and plunge his audience into dark-

ness. All this is but for a moment, for the Lord will ensure the preaching of the Word of God.

Christ controls the affairs of men. History is plastic to his purpose. Much may be done by men against his will, but nothing can ever be done apart from his will. He molds the deeds of men and nations to dovetail into his plan.

He controls the church and protects it. He is over every rule and authority and power and lordship and every name that is named, in this age and in the coming age (Eph. 1:20–23). Everything is under his feet and in subjection to him. And God *gave* him to the church—as Head over everything. This Head has no equal! The church is safe in his hands, never to be snatched away from him (John 10:28), and the church is aided by him in the work of evangelism.

Jesus Christ has the world at his feet and the church in his hands.

Where do you stand? Reason suggests the folly of opposing him. Conscience suggests the folly of trying to evade him. The Holy Spirit speaks to you and calls you.

Confess your sin. *Admit it!* This is the last thing you are willing to do, and it has to be dragged out of you. Admit that God is right and you are wrong. Admit that you are a sinner. Turn away from your proud and sinful self. Hand yourself over to Jesus.

Flee to Christ. And tell him: "For me, O Jesus, you are Lord."

10

The Significance of Pentecost
Dennis Franklin Kinlaw

> And when the Day of Pentecost had come, they were all together in one place. And suddenly there came from heaven a noise like a violent, rushing wind, and it filled the whole house where they were sitting. And there appeared to them tongues as of fire distributing themselves, and they rested on each one of them. And they were all filled with the Holy Spirit and began to speak with other tongues, as the Spirit was giving them utterance.
>
> Acts 2:1–4 (NASB)

Biblical religion has a special interest in time and history. They are the milieu in which man lives. They are the arena in which God reveals himself and redeems man. Some times are more important than others. They are the days when God draws near to do special work.

Every good student knows that God is always everywhere. But that has to do with existence, not redemption. He gives everything its being. Without his sustaining presence nothing would exist. As the writer of Hebrews says, God "upholds all things by the word of His power . . ." (Heb. 1:3).

But existence and redemption are two different things. God is always everywhere, sustaining all. He is not always everywhere all-present. Some exist outside his redemptive working. But there are times when he comes with redeeming purpose and power. These are the great times. And human history has its share of these.

The Old Testament records such special days. One was the occasion when God drew near to a man named Abram in the city of Ur and called him to follow him. Human history still feels the impact of that day. Another such day was the one when God delivered Israel from bondage in the exodus from Egypt. There came into existence then a people whose very national life was due to the redemptive work of God. The days when God appeared to Moses on the mountain to give him the law were special, too. Now definition and content were given to the term "the people of God." Israel knew, and the world could know, what it means to belong to the living God.

The New Testament has its special days, too. Christmas is the first. It corresponds in the New Testament to that Old Testament day in Ur. The Eternal Son left heaven and came to this darkened and lost world so that it might have light and salvation, just as Abram left Ur to find God's will and hope for mankind.

The weekend that included Calvary and the resurrection from the tomb compares remarkably to the exodus from Egypt. In the one, God gave the world a people, his people, who would light the way for the world. In the cross and resurrection, God has given to his people the knowledge of how they and that larger world are to be redeemed. The Way and the Truth had appeared in flesh (John 14:6). A door was now opened—*the* Door for all people.

That, however, is not all. A third sacred occasion occurred, an occasion the church and the world tend to ignore, since most churches climax their year with Easter. But the biblical fact is that Pentecost is the most climactic day in holy history up to the present moment. The next such day will be the day of Christ's return.

It was in all these great events that God revealed himself and redeemed men and women. The full understanding of the meaning of these acts of God would come later as the Scriptures were written under divine inspiration. The "saving acts of God," however, were concluded at Pentecost.

What, then, is the significance of Pentecost? We must look primarily to Luke and Peter for our understanding.

A New Understanding of God

Pentecost was a climax in God's revelation of himself. This day, along with Advent and Holy Week, lets us know that God is even bigger than we thought.

The greatness of the Old Testament lies in its revelation of the nature of Israel's God. The prophet Isaiah had wondered to whom God could be compared and who could understand him (Isa. 40:18, 25, 28). This God was the transcendent and sovereign Creator of all. Other religions had difficulty drawing a sharp line between man, nature, and the realm of the divine. The continuity was considered so great that almost any earthly material or form could be used to represent the divine. For paganism, the divine itself turned out to be simply natural forces that were personified and worshiped.

Israel knew that its God was different. He was *one* God, and he was above and beyond the creation. He must not be confused with the creation. No creaturely material or form could symbolize him, and the line between a creature and its source was such that no creature could cross it. God was God, and creature was creature.

But then Jesus of Nazareth appeared. He did things no mortal can do. He said things no human should say. He assumed rights and privileges no creature should assume. He was different from all who preceded him. He was prophetic, yet greater than a prophet. He was wise, but he was more than Solomon. His enemies said that he was "making himself equal with God" (John 5:18). Simon Peter said, "You are the Christ . . ." (Matt. 16:16). Even the doubting apostle Thomas called him "my Lord and my God" (John 20:28). A Gentile centurion said it best at the cross: "Truly this man was the Son of God!" (Mark 15:39).

His best friends were Jews who never questioned the Old Testament view of God as "one" and as "other." But when Jesus rose from the tomb and ascended, they felt that in seeing Jesus they had seen God and that in touching him they had touched the Deity. The God of Abraham and Moses was a God beyond and above all. They knew that somehow, in Jesus, he had been *with* them. The doctrine of the two-fold nature of Christ, the Christian belief in the incarnation, was now inevitable.

But there is more. The day of Pentecost came. A divine effusion was poured out on Peter and his friends in the Upper Room. That charisma brought an intellectual illumination with the effusion. Peter saw things he had never anticipated.

Peter now remembered the baptism of Jesus, when the Spirit of God descended upon Jesus. He remembered how the Baptist had declared this to be the sign of Jesus' messiahship. He remembered how Jesus himself had attributed his own power to that same Spirit. He recalled how Jesus had promised that after his ascension he would send that same Spirit to his friends (John 15:26). And now Peter knew that promise had been fulfilled. That same Spirit had filled him and his friends. The Spirit of Christ, the Spirit of God himself, had come to them. The God beyond, who in Jesus had been *with* them, was now in his Spirit *within* them. They had no term for the Trinity, but the experience that made this language ultimately necessary was theirs. They could now speak of the Father who sent his Son in Jesus and who had now given himself in his Spirit. Yes! God was bigger than they had anticipated. The revelatory events necessary to reveal that were now complete.

A New Understanding of Salvation

Pentecost meant that God's salvation was better than the followers of Jesus had dreamed.

Israel was a privileged people. Jesus had told the Samaritan woman that salvation was of the Jews (John 4:22). They were the people upon whom the light had shined. It had come at Sinai in the law. It came also in prophet and wise man. Israel possessed the temple, the priesthood, the sacrifices, and the sacred books. In these things they were the envy of the wisest and best in the pagan world. But their hearts had yearned for more. Now that "more" had come.

The New Testament is very clear in speaking about the difference between the old covenant and the new. The old covenant is spoken of as promise (Acts 26:6–7; Rom. 15:8). The writer of the Hebrews speaks of symbols and shadows (Heb. 8:5; 10:1). Paul speaks of types and allegory (Rom. 5:14; Gal. 4:24). Peter identifies the new age as "these last times" (1 Peter 1:20, NASB). Here one thinks not so much of conclusion as fulfillment. The day of preparation is over. The period of childhood and training—with its limitations, its restrictions, and its obscurities—is over. The fullness of time has now come, with its realities that were only foreshadowed in the old covenant.

It is a better day. Jesus, God's eternal Son, not Aaron's descendants, is now our high priest. Our salvation rests not on the blood of bulls and goats, but upon the sacrifice of Christ, God's own Son. Intimate access to God is now not only the privilege of a high priest once a year, but of every believer always. Human intermediaries are no longer necessary. The true and living way is open to all. The law is now no longer a code written on tables of stone contained in the ark of the covenant in the innermost recess of the temple. That law can now be written within the human heart so that the dynamic for obedience is not external but from deep within. The delight in the law of God of which the Psalmist sang (Ps. 1:2) can now be everyone's experience. The shadows have passed, and the reality has come. A new universalism now reigns. God's best is available to all.

Just as under the old covenant Israel enjoyed a privileged place among the nations, so there were certain ones within Israel who had enjoyed special privileges. The greatest of all of God's gifts from early in Israel's history was the gift of the Spirit.

It was the Spirit that made a king a true king. Saul learned the truth of this when the Spirit was taken from him and placed upon the un-crowned David. It was the Spirit that made a man a prophet. The anointing oil upon the priest spoke symbolically of the need of the priest for that same Spirit so that he might fulfill his unique role. But most of all it was the Messiah who was to be marked by that divine charisma. His very title meant "anointed." And so the Davids and the Aarons and the Elijahs and their like under the old covenant knew the special anointing of God.

Now a new day has come. God's best gift is for *all*. He is for the young as well as for the old. He is for the female as well as the male. He is for the servant as well as for the master. He is for the Gentile as well as for the Jew. The days of special privilege are over. God's best is available for all. Regality, priestly access, the prophetic gift, and wisdom itself are the privilege of every believer. God's kingdom is a royal priesthood, and that kingdom of anointed priests has come (Rev. 1:6).

There is now a new permanency in the believer's relationship to the Holy Spirit as well. Under the old covenant, the gift of the Spirit was for special people in particular roles and often for special occasions. The relationship of the Spirit to the judges of Israel like Gideon and Samson is illustrative. Now the possession of the Spirit is not related to special roles or seasons. It is a privilege that results from the believer's relationship to Christ. The Spirit is the special gift of the Father offered to all who belong to Christ. And he is offered permanently. The transitory has passed. The abiding has come.

A New Sense of Vocation

If Pentecost meant a new understanding of God and a new understanding of salvation, it also meant a new sense of vocation. The task of the disciples was more serious than they had anticipated.

Early in his ministry Jesus had spoken to the Twelve about being fishers of men. Later he called them to be with him, to preach and to exercise authority over the demonic. They were his servants. He was their Master.

After the confession of Peter that Jesus was the Christ, the relationship began to deepen. Now that they knew his identity, he began to speak to them about the mystery of his mission, about the cross. They had difficulty understanding this, but they could not miss the fact that his destiny and theirs were becoming more entwined.

As the cross drew near, Jesus made it clear that they were not just servants. He called them friends (John 15:14–15). He opened to them an intimacy with himself and with his Father. What belonged to the Father belonged to him. Now he said that what belonged to him was also theirs (John 16:15). Their relationship had become so intimate that he used language of identity like that which he used of his relationship to the Father (John 14:20; 15:9–10). If they received him, they received the Father. If they missed him, they missed the Father. Anyone who received them, received him and his Father (John 13:20). Intimacy had become oneness.

It was, however, a oneness of vocation as well as a unity of love. Jesus now projected upon them the purpose for which the Father had sent him. What he was to the Father, they were to him. But now, what he was to them, they were to be to the world. As the Father had sent him, so he now sent them (John 17:18).

The fulfillment of Christ's task necessitated the cross. So he told them that the fulfillment of their vocation would mean a cross for them (Matt. 16:24; John 16:2). Who is sufficient for such a load?

It was Easter evening in the privacy of a locked room when Jesus said, "Receive the Holy Spirit" (John 20:22). The dynamic of his life must be theirs if they were to do his work. Now the anointing has come. The Messiah's anointing is theirs to do the Messiah's work. What a story! What a vocation! What a partnership! And the redemption of a lost world hangs on it. He has given them the task, and he has also given them the provision for effectiveness, the same Spirit that filled and empowered him. As he witnessed, now they can witness in word and life.

Pentecost was an epochal day. The days of preparation were over. The last days had come, the days of fulfillment, the days of salvation for the whole world.

There is no question that those of us who live in the Pentecostal Age are people of privilege. God's great redemptive and revelatory acts are behind us. We have the additional advantage of a concluded canon. The Scriptures are ours to help us understand the full character of the revelation and the redemption. That privilege is obvious whenever we read the Book of Acts and compare the apostles' knowledge of God and the power of God at work in them with the knowledge and the experience of their counterparts in the Old Testament.

A haunting question, however, remains—as, today we read the Book of Acts and compare the knowledge of God and the experience of his presence that the New Testament believers had with our own. We see a difference, and we wonder. Does privilege guarantee full possession? Is it possible to live in a period of higher privilege at a lower level of grace? Are there many of us who know more of the partial and the transitory, of shadow and type, than we do of the full and the enduring and the real?

An affirmative answer to that question should not shock anyone who knows that grace is never mechanical or automatic. Time is not what sanctifies and satisfies. It is penitence and faith that enable us to receive the Spirit provided. Some people under old-covenant limitation seem to have experienced more of a new-covenant privilege than many of us who have new-covenant opportunity. Could that be why we are still so far from fulfilling the calling our Lord left us? The power is in the Spirit, not in us. Jesus made that clear. The flesh profits nothing; it is the Spirit that gives life (John 6:63).

Is this why Paul pleads for believers to be filled with the Spirit (Eph. 5:18)? If the provision is fullness, the partial is not enough. May God help us, his church, to match possession with privilege. Is his word to us still, "Did you receive the Holy Spirit?" (Acts 19:2).

11

The Trinity and the Gospel
James I. Packer

Jesus answered, "I tell you the truth, no one can enter the kingdom of God unless he is born of water and the Spirit."

John 3:5 (NIV)

Why is it that so many churches, schools, and colleges bear the name *Trinity*? I once taught at a British school called Trinity, and some people thought that its name came from the fact that three colleges had united to form it. But that, though true, was not the reason. We took the name Trinity College because Trinity is the Christian word for describing the Christian God.

The English Prayer Book of 1662, on which I was brought up, linked liturgical direction with tutorial instruction on many matters, and the Trinity was one of them. Accordingly, it directed that on Trinity Sunday, seven days after Pentecost, the Athanasian Creed should replace the Apostles' Creed in morning worship. Now this was not a very bright idea. The Athanasian Creed, which is a five-minute-long technical statement about the Trinity, takes a lot of unpacking; and if not unpacked, it bewilders. It contains lines like "the Father incomprehensible, the Son incomprehensible: and the Holy Ghost incomprehensible"—which once, it is said, goaded a chorister into hissing, "And the whole thing incomprehensible!" I doubt whether much save mystification ever resulted from these yearly recitations, and the Prayer Book's insistence on them was something for which I could only, at best, give two cheers, perhaps on reflection, only one. But the Prayer

Book then made up for this leaden requirement by a stroke of real genius. It set as its Trinity Sunday Gospel Jesus' conversation with Nicodemus in John 3. Have you ever thought of that conversation as a revelation of what faith in the Trinity is all about? It is so, as we are going to see.

"But what do we mean by faith in the Trinity?" asks someone (and I do not blame anyone for asking; the fact is that most worshipers nowadays are far from sure). Well, as stated in the Athanasian Creed, if I may hark back to that for a moment, it is the belief that God is as truly three as he is one; that the unity of his being, his "substance," as the creed calls it, is tripersonal; that the Father, the Son, and the Holy Spirit are coequal and coeternal, uncreated and inseparable, undivided though distinguishable. This is a truth that becomes clear when Jesus in the Gospels indicates, on the one hand, that though he is divine and to be worshiped, he is not the same person as the Father, whose will he does and to whom he prays—and then indicates, on the other hand, that the Holy Spirit, who will come as his deputy, is a further divine person on the same footing as himself. It is this truth that the Athanasian Creed is spelling out.

"But why," asks the inquirer, "does it use such long-winded laborious language?"

For a very good reason indeed. The purpose of what the creed so carefully says about the coeternity and coequality of the three persons within a single substance is defensive. The aim is to rule out erroneous ideas, of which there are always many when the Trinity is under discussion. There is, for instance, the idea that God is like the late great Peter Sellers in Dr. *Strangelove*, one person playing several roles in a single story. We actually project that idea every time we tell a Sunday-school class that as each lump of sugar has six sides, so the one God has three faces and identities. How common an illustration that is—and how heretical! I once saw a cartoon of a moth-eaten clergyman (Anglican, of course) telling a congregation of two old ladies, "I know what you're thinking—Sabellianism!" The caption was meant, of course, as a joke (you realized that? good). But Sabellianism is the historic name for the idea I have just mentioned, and it is, in fact, widespread.

Then there is the idea that Jesus and the Spirit are not personally divine, but are God's two top creatures doing top jobs. Jehovah's Witnesses think that. There is also the idea that the Father, the Son, and the Holy Spirit are three gods whose solidarity in action masks the fact that they are not one in being. Mormons think that. A further false idea is that the Son is God of a weaker strain than the Father and that the Spirit's divinity is weaker still. All these ideas had a run for their money in the early church before being condemned as heresies. All of them still pop up from time to time today.

What this shows is that the idea of the Trinity is one of the hardest thoughts round which the human mind has ever been asked to wrap itself. It is far easier to get it wrong than to get it right. So if it were proposed that the Athanasian Creed should be not just dropped from public worship, but removed from the Prayer Book entirely, I should vote against the motion. The Athanasian Creed is historically a classic witness against unbiblical distortions and denials of the triunity of our God, and such witnesses will always be needed.

When, however, we turn to what Jesus said to Nicodemus, we find faith in the Trinity presented in quite a different light—not now as the linchpin of orthodox belief (which nonetheless it is), but as, literally and precisely, the sinner's way of salvation. How does Jesus' teaching here do this? Let me show you how.

Ten years ago, in a 90-degree heat wave, a student group led me to the top of a 3,000-foot mountain outside Vancouver. The climb was rugged and the sweat was copious, but the view was glorious. When afterwards I asked where we had been, I was told I had climbed the Squamish Chief. I climbed it, however, without knowing what it was or what to call it. That is my illustration of how John 3:1–15, which we rightly think of as a passage proclaiming the gospel, introduces us to the Trinity. As one learns the Christian gospel and enters by faith into the riches of fellowship with God that it holds forth, one is, in fact, mastering the mystery of the Triune God. We might say he is climbing the mountain called the Trinity all the time, whether he realizes it or not. Jesus' conversation with Nicodemus makes this very clear. Look at it with me now.

Nicodemus, a senior Jewish ruler and theologian, a man as eminent as an archbishop, a cardinal, or a distinguished professor today, has come to meet Jesus, the novice preacher from the Galilean backwoods, who is in Jerusalem, it seems, for the first time since his ministry started. Being older (he appears to call himself an old man in verse 4 and was probably twice Jesus' age), Nicodemus speaks first. His opening words are kind words, words of affirmation and welcome. "Rabbi [teacher]," he says, giving the young preacher a title of honour straight away, "we [that is, "my colleagues and I," Jerusalem's top people] know you are a teacher who has come from God. For no one could perform the miraculous signs you are doing if God were not with him" (v. 2, NIV). As if to say: "I am sure, Jesus, that you are wondering whether we of the religious establishment accept you and approve of what you are doing and regard you as one of us. Well now, I am here to tell you that we do, and we shall be happy to have you as a regular member of our discussion circle [the Jerusalem Theological Society, as we might call it]. Come and join us!" Such was the burden of Nicodemus's speech.

Do you see, now, what Nicodemus was doing under all that politeness? By treating Jesus as a recruit for the Jewish establishment, he was patronizing the Son of God! But Jesus did not accept patronage from Nicodemus or anyone else while he was on earth, just as he will not accept your patronage or mine, now that he reigns in heaven. It is for us to bow down before him, not to expect him to bow down before us, whoever we are. So Jesus does not respond by thanking Nicodemus for his kind words. He strikes a different note and tells his eminent visitor that without being born again, one cannot see the kingdom of God. When Nicodemus expresses bewilderment, Jesus amplifies his meaning in the words of our text: "I tell you the truth, no one can enter the kingdom of God unless he is born of water and the Spirit." Then he explains that natural and spiritual birth are two different things and concludes: "You should not be surprised at my saying, 'You [plural: "you, Nicodemus, and all those whom you represent"] must be born again'" (v. 7).

Three Persons

I ask you, now, to notice two things. The first is that *there are three persons* mentioned in verse 5, which is our text. There is the "I" of "I tell you the truth," the speaker, Jesus himself—God's "one and only Son," as John, in 1:14, has already called him, and as the beloved verse 16 of this chapter will call him again. There is "God," the One whom Jesus called Father and taught his disciples to call Father—God whose kingdom Jesus is announcing. And there is the Holy Spirit, through whose power in new creation one must start life all over again, if one is ever to see and enter the kingdom. These are the three persons of the divine Trinity who are our special concern now. This is the first of a number of places in John's Gospel where all three are spoken of together.

Three Stages

The second thing I ask you to notice is that *there are three stages* in the flow of Jesus' response to Nicodemus. We may set them out as follows.

Do you want to see and enter the kingdom of God? Then you must be born again, of water and the Spirit (vv. 3–10).

What is the kingdom of God? The whole New Testament makes clear that it is not a territorial realm (unless you think of the human heart as a territory), but a personal relationship. The kingdom exists in any life where God is made King and Jesus the Savior is acknowledged as Lord. The relationship brings salvation from sin and Satan and spiritual death. Jesus bestows forgiveness of sins, adoption into God's family, and the joy of eternal life on all who entrust their destiny to him and give him the love and loyalty of their hearts. To this new relationship, the path—the only path, as Jesus explains to Nicodemus—is new birth "You must be born again." Without new birth one can neither see nor enter the kingdom of God.

What is this new birth? What does it mean to be "born of water and the Spirit?" Briefly, and with due respect to other views (for the ground here is much fought over), I state what seems to me to be quite clear. All explanations of this key phrase that posit a contrast between "water" (John's baptism, Christian baptism, or the waters of physical birth) and "the Spirit" are on the wrong track. "Water" and "the Spirit" are two aspects of one reality; namely, God's renewal of the fallen and unresponsive human heart. Jesus is referring back to these two aspects, the purifying and the energizing aspects, just as they were set forth in God's promise to renew Israelite hearts in Ezekiel 36:25–27:

> I will sprinkle clean *water* on you . . . I will cleanse you from all your impurities and from all your idols. I will give you a new heart and put a new spirit in you. . . . I will put *my Spirit* in you and move you to follow my decrees and be careful to keep my laws [NIV, italics mine].

Sinners who are naturally and habitually in rebellion against God, as were the Jews of Ezekiel's day and of Jesus' day—and as we are, too, with the rest of the human race—need an inward cleansing and a change of heart that only God can bring about. Of this inward transformation, "new birth" is a two-word illustration—a parable, in fact. The change is so radical and drastic that it constitutes a totally fresh start to one's life. That is what makes the picture of being born again so fitting a way to describe it.

Why am I sure that Jesus' words about water and the Spirit look back to Ezekiel? Because of the way Jesus chides Nicodemus in verse 10. "You are Israel's teacher," he says, "and do you not understand these things?" Jesus is implying that such ignorance is shameful in a Jewish teacher. But the rebuke only has point if the things Nicodemus did not understand were things that the Jewish Scriptures clearly set forth.

Thus Jesus lays it down that only through new birth can Nicodemus, or you, or I, or anyone else, come into the kingdom of God. This leads to the second stage in his flow of thought.

Do you want to be born again? Then you must be willing to learn from Jesus Christ (vv. 11–13).

You have met people whose behavior leads you to say, "You can't tell them anything." In verse 11, Jesus says that Nicodemus and his peers are behaving that way towards him and his disciples: "I tell you the truth, we speak of what we know, and we testify to what we have seen, but still you people do not accept our testimony" (NIV). By Nicodemus's own admission, the Jewish theologians did not know about the new birth and God's present kingdom, but they had not so far shown any willingness to accept teaching on these things from Jesus, the country preacher. Yet Jesus was in reality the Son of man—that is, the Messiah—who had come down from heaven, as verse 13 declares, in order to make these things known!

Before we condemn those Jewish leaders, however, we should ask ourselves if we are any wiser than they were at this point. Do we let Jesus teach us spiritual things? Have we let him teach us our own need of new birth? Will we let him teach us the way into God's kingdom? This is the topic to which he now moves on. Hear him well, then, as he utters his final challenging words about it.

Are you willing to learn from Jesus Christ? Then let him teach you to trust in him and his cross for your salvation (vv. 14–15).

Once more Jesus refers to the Old Testament—this time to the story in Numbers 21:6–9, which tells how Israelites suffering snakebite were told to look at a brass snake that Moses, at God's command, had put up on a pole; and those who looked lived. "Just as Moses lifted up the snake in the desert," says Jesus "so the Son of Man must be lifted up, that everyone who believes in him may have eternal life" (NIV). The final message to Nicodemus, and to us, is this: Believe in Jesus—that is, trust in him, rely on him, tell him that he is your only hope, embrace him as your Savior—and your sins will be forgiven, your sickness of spirit healed, and your uncleanness before God washed away. Then you will know that you, too, have been born again.

The statement of verses 14 and 15, pointing as it does to Jesus' cross as the means of our salvation, is the purest gospel, as is the beloved sixteenth verse that follows it: "For God so loved the world that he gave his one and only Son, that whoever believes in him shall not perish but have eternal life" (NIV). In learning the good news from these words, we are on familiar ground. But what I am asking you to notice now is that the entire conversation with Nicodemus presents us with profound teaching about the Trinity also, by setting before us the person and work both of God's Son and of God's Spirit. Jesus, we learn, is the God-sent, divine-human sin-bearer, who by his cross secured eternal life for us. The Spirit is the divine regenerator who by transforming our inner disposition, and in that sense changing our nature, enables us to experience the life of the kingdom of God. Without the Son and the Spirit there can be no salvation for anyone.

One Truth

What it amounts to, then, is that in this passage, as in many more throughout the New Testament, the truths of the Holy Trinity and of sovereign saving grace prove to be not two truths, but one. The doctrine of salvation is the good news of the Father's giving us his Son to redeem us and his Spirit to renew us. The doctrine of the Trinity is the good news of three divine persons working together to raise us into spiritual life and bring us to the glory of God's kingdom. The Athanasian Creed guards this good news in the way that fences round a field guard growing crops from preying animals. Such fences are needed, but they do not have equal value with the crops they protect, and such value as they have derives from those crops themselves. Trinitarian orthodoxy, in other words, has value only as it sustains and safeguards evangelical faith.

Two conclusions follow for us, therefore.

First: Do not dismiss the doctrine of the Trinity as so much useless lumber for the mind. If the place of any of the three persons is misconceived or denied, the gospel falls. Jehovah's Witnesses and Mormons, and those liberal Protestants for whom the personal deity of the Son and the Spirit is suspect, can never state the gospel rightly because they think of the Godhead wrongly. Clear confession of the Trinity is foundational. The gospel proclaims precisely the joint saving action of the three persons, and it is lost as soon as one's hold on their distinct divine personhood slackens.

Second: Let the doctrine of the Trinity keep your understanding of the gospel in good shape. Let it remind you to give equal emphasis in your thinking and your witness to the sovereign initiative of the Father who planned salvation, the atoning sacrifice of the Son who obtained salvation, and the mighty power of the Spirit who applies salvation. Let it prompt you to lay equal stress on the love of each in the work of grace. The late Dr. D. Martyn Lloyd-Jones used to tell how early in his ministry a senior pastor said to him that having listened to several of Lloyd-Jones's sermons, he could not make out whether "the Doctor" was a Quaker or a hyper-Calvinist, because all the sermons centered on either the Spirit's work in the human heart or the sovereignty of God in salvation, and so little was said about the cross and faith in the crucified Savior. "The Doctor" quickly took the point! But there are many preachers today, and other Christians, too, who in their thinking and speaking stress either the cross all the time and say all too little about the Spirit, or stress God's saving plan or the Spirit's renewing work all the time and say all too little about the cross. Take care! False proportions in our doctrine are the beginning of false doctrine itself.

So let the truth of the Trinity keep you balanced at this point. Make it a matter of conscience to do full justice in your thought, your speech, and your worship, both in public and in private, to the love, wisdom, power, and achievement of each divine person separately, as well as of all three together. Then your theology will benefit, and your soul will prosper, and your whole life will express, as it should, the spirit of this old and precious doxology with which I close:

Glory be to the Father, and to the Son, and to the Holy Spirit; As it was in the beginning, is now, and ever shall be, world without end. Amen.

12

The Saints
John Guest

Paul, an apostle of Christ Jesus by the will of God, To the saints who are also faithful in Christ Jesus.

Ephesians 1:1

There is a tremendous interest today in life after death, or, as one author has written, "life after life." All kinds of studies, purported to be scientific, have been made of people who, after being declared dead, were resuscitated and have shared what they have experienced in those moments of death. We have all probably either read some of these studies or perhaps even seen some of these people interviewed on television.

It is a crying shame that within the church there is a nebulous attitude toward life beyond the grave. For when we recite the Apostles' Creed and the Nicene Creed, we state that we believe in eternal life, that is, a forever life. We state that we believe in the resurrection of the dead and the communion of saints. As we celebrate All Saints' Day, it is tragic that the agnosticism of the world around us, the commitment to knowing nothing for sure, has eroded our confidence in the Christian gospel, which promises everlasting life to every believer in Christ.

Let us examine together what the Bible means when it speaks of saints. First, when the word *saint* is used in the New Testament, it almost always refers not to someone who has died, but to someone who is living. Yet we tend to think of saints as dead Christian heroes. We depict them in stained-glass windows, make statues of them, and remem-

99

ber them on special days, as if they were history. But the Bible describes every living Christian believer as a "saint."

Look at Paul's words to the church at Ephesus. He begins: "Paul, an apostle of Christ Jesus by the will of God, To the saints who are also faithful in Christ Jesus." Every Christian believer, according to the Bible, is a saint. I could greet you at the door of the church and call you Saint Eleanor, or Saint George, or Saint Mary, because of your faith in Jesus Christ.

Notice, and this is very important, that those whom the Bible calls saints were not perfect. Have you ever realized that nearly every one of Paul's letters was written to deal with *problems* in the church? The early church was not perfect. The first Christians were not perfect. In fact, every Epistle was written because of their imperfections. Paul and the other apostles wrote letters to teach the early church what ought to be believed and how Christians ought to behave. They were by no means perfect.

The next thing I want us to grasp is that *in Jesus Christ* we have been made saints. When God looks at a Christian, he sees someone who looks like Jesus. We find this very hard to believe because we know that we are not at all like Jesus. But as we have set our lives within the boundaries of the grace of Jesus Christ, so we are robed in his righteousness. Despite what is underneath that robe, what God sees is the righteousness of Jesus vesting every Christian believer.

So will it be in heaven at the end of time. The Book of Revelation describes the heavenly congregation gathered for worship. Do you remember the question raised by one of the elders about those who were robed in white? "Who are these, clothed in white robes, and whence have they come?" Then, answering his own question, the elder continued, "These are they who have come out of the great tribulation; they have washed their robes and made them white in the blood of the Lamb" (Rev. 7:13–14).

In other words, these are ordinary sinful men and women who have been made righteous through Jesus Christ, who died for them. They stand in perfect innocence and beauty, worshiping God with open and pure hearts, not because they became pure by their own effort, but because when they gave themselves to Christ in faith, they were clothed with his purity. The blood of Jesus Christ cleanses us from *all* sin (1 John 1:7). God sees us as we are in Christ.

How, then, do we become in ourselves what God sees us to be in

Christ? That process is called sanctification. It is a day-by-day process of increasingly becoming, or growing up into, what God has already made us in Jesus Christ.

The biblical imagery of "adoption" helps us to understand this. In the first chapter of Ephesians, Paul talks about saints as being adopted (Eph. 1:5, KJV). The only way we become part of the family of God is to be adopted. We are not naturally children in God's family; we must be adopted into his family. Because of our faith in Jesus Christ, we are given the authority to be called by his name: "Christians." As a *Christian*, I have been adopted into the family of the Lord Jesus, bear the family name, and, as far as the Father is concerned, I look like Jesus Christ.

Some of you have adopted children when they were several years old. At first, they didn't fit naturally into your family. But gradually they began to take on the family attitude and the family disposition. They belong to the family. You have given them your name. You treat them as if they are yours. And more and more, day by day, they are coming to reflect the character of your family. Similarly, we are to become more and more like Jesus Christ.

The fifth chapter of Matthew's Gospel describes the attitudes of the family of Jesus Christ (vv. 1–11). They are called the Beatitudes, the "beautiful attitudes." These are the attitudes of the kingdom of God, and we should be growing up into them. Are we merciful? Do we forgive as we have been forgiven? Or do we bury people with their failures? Do we continually remind them of how they have let us down? Do we begin to act as if they are no longer trustworthy because they have failed us?

Are we peacemakers? Most of us are warlike. We need to begin to cultivate the peacemaker attitude. Jesus is our model. He is not a peace-at-any-price sort of person, who would give up both his own rights and the rights of others to preserve his life. Rather, he sacrificed his life for us. It is not possible to be a peacemaker without being merciful. That is what we should grow up to be.

We need encouragement. The disparity between what God has made us in Jesus Christ and what we perceive ourselves to be is often great. A student said to me recently, "There are so many areas in my life that are wrong, I am really discouraged. I don't know where to begin to put things right." I feel like that myself most of the time. By the time I have met with my staff, talked with my wife, been put straight by my kids, then passed a few parishioners on the street, I feel like a dead loss. Isn't that true of all of us? It seems there is so much to put right that we don't know where to begin.

The encouragement is this: God has given us his Holy Spirit. We are working in harness with the Spirit of God. God has not turned us loose and said, "Now look, I have my name on you. Shape up and act accordingly." He says, "I have given you my Spirit, who will empower you to live my way."

Let me give you an illustration. Suppose you wanted to be a great athlete, a Mary Lou Retton, for example. Watching her perform gymnastics is like watching perfection. If you wanted to perform like Mary Lou Retton, you would watch tapes of her performing to study her style so that you might copy her technique. But you know as well as I do that no matter how much you practiced, you could never perform as she does. You are not Mary Lou and do not have her natural abilities.

Some, however, think that being a Christian is watching a performance by Jesus Christ and then trying to emulate it. Not at all. Jesus Christ offers to come and indwell us. Then, by the influence and power of his Spirit, we are able to perform like him. The Holy Spirit of God works from within, helping us to be conformed more and more to the image of Jesus Christ.

We are "saints," then, if we have given our lives to Jesus Christ. And because his Holy Spirit lives within us, we can live a Christlike life.

Part **2**

Other Special Days

13

All Things Will Be New
James Earl Massey

> *And he who sat upon the throne said, "Behold, I make all things new."*
> *Also he said, "Write this, for these words are trustworthy and true."*
> Revelation 21:5

This text holds a promise from God about the future. Hebrew Christians reading the Book of Revelation took this to be a reminding word about what the Old Testament prophets had heralded concerning the renewal of history. Gathering the visionary themes of those prophets, John restated them for a new generation of believers, a group of world-weary saints who needed a fresh word of cheer during hard times under Roman rule. Having dealt with the privileges of salvation and the reason for Christian hope, John was about to close out the Revelation. He did so by giving a picture of the future, as God would make it: "Behold, I make all things new." A divine happening is expected, a happening that will shape a future whose details are determined and controlled by God alone. The promise is about a future that will fulfill us. It will be a *complete life.*

"Behold, I make all things new." This is a revelational word. This is a divine promise. The God who has been acting *within* history has promised to act *beyond* it to make all things new.

The Answer to Hope

"All things new." This divine promise appeals to an ancient and deep-seated human hope. Martin Luther King, Jr., was speaking out of

105

that hope when he said, "Humanity is waiting for something other than blind imitation of the past."

All of us have deep inward yearnings to which this promise speaks. Our hearts vibrate under its impact. We all know that this promise from God makes all the sense in the world, and it helps this world make sense.

As for the idea of renewal, it is as old as man's experience of brokenness. The desire to see utter newness is as old as human failure; there has always been a strong wish in the human heart to start out fresh again. Man's desire for renewal is reflected in his earliest records and it has influenced most forms of religious life. The desire for renewal is also seen in the many theories about how renewal will come. Most of these theories vary one from another in certain features, but they also overlap at the point of believing that this world is amenable to change and that a difference needs to be made in the human scene.

We are conditioned by nature to desire change and to make it. This is the human story. But that story sadly shows a prolonged imitation of the past. It is the story of limitations, failures, and errors in our attempts at tinkering with life. Thus the painfulness in our human struggle: the old order refuses to yield to our will to change it, and we realize that we are trapped in the prison of sameness—the same selfishness, suffering, sadness, personal sin, and societal madness.

Whither goes our world? It is to this question that God's promise to his people speaks: "Behold, I make all things new." Life as it is transcends our human control, and the future we need is beyond our human shaping. God alone can effect the renewal of all things. He has promised to do so.

Creation Fulfilled

"All things new." This promise should not be misunderstood as meaning a total break with everything that experience in this world has involved. This promise does not involve a shift so total that every link with the past will be broken. The promise is rather about a renewed scene of life. God promises a change in the state of affairs. The promise is about a setting in which all creation will find itself fulfilled. In Romans 8:18–21, Paul was dealing with the same expectation:

> I consider that the sufferings of this present time are not worth comparing with the glory that is to be revealed to us. For the creation waits with eager longing for the revealing of the sons of God; for the creation

was subjected to futility, not of its own will but by the will of him who subjected it in hope; *because the creation itself will be set free from its bondage to decay and obtain the glorious liberty of the children of God* [italics mine].

Paul was writing about the renewal God has promised us. Like John, Paul knew that life in the world to come will mean the fulfillment of the best we have known in the past. The Greek word John used here for "new" makes this quite clear. It was the word normally used to express the continuation of something, but in an altered form. The life to come will have continuity with what was, but there will be a contrast, because it will be different in its quality.

What we have before us in this promise from God to make "all things new" is the establishment of the conditions for a glorified life, a life of unhindered community with God and one another. The succeeding verses in the passage tell us so. "Behold, the dwelling of God is with men. He will dwell with them, and they shall be his people, and God himself will be with them; he will wipe away every tear from their eyes, and death shall be no more, neither shall there be mourning nor crying nor pain any more, for the former things have passed away" (Rev. 21:3–4).

God has promised to make this happen. It will not happen in Utopia, a "no-place"; it will happen in a real place and for a resurrected people who will have been made qualitatively new to match that place. John called that place the "new earth." It will be a full life. It will be the final life, a life that is substantial and sacred. It will be a life in which pain and death have no place. It will be a life with an ethical perfection that rules out sin. It will be a fulfilled life that has no place in it for sorrow, tears, or a feeling of loss. Call the process that brings it what you will—renovation, renewal, transformation, the new creation— its presence will be more important than the process by which it comes.

Think of it! We are going to have a new world by the will of God. Here again is his word: "Behold, I make all things new." This is an encouraging word for all of us who are painfully involved in history, disturbed about it, and hungry for the best that our hearts tell us ought to be.

A Present and Future Reality

The promise that "*all* things" will be made new implies that we have already seen the renewal of *some* things. And that is the case! God has acted in history again and again to show his power and to help us. That God is a change-maker is the main message in our Bible. Beginning with creation, continuing with the way he shaped and guided the life and fortunes of the Hebrews, the sending of Jesus, and the formation of the church whose story fills the last half of the Bible—all through the pages of Scripture we see God at work with his people in mind, eager to ease their weariness and grant them benefits from above.

Yes, aspects of renewal are a present reality! Those who have been "born again" know this. They know it in their minds, which glow with brighter awareness because of a renewing knowledge of the truth. They know it in their spirits, which rejoice in freedom from a previous bondage to sin. They know it in their hearts, where they daily worship God and bless his name with a joy known only by those "who have been forgiven much."

Yes, inward renewal is a present reality! We realize this again and again as our troubled moods, fears, and anxieties subside or die when we worship and pray. An active sense of God's presence and purpose does creative, renewing service to the whole self. That is how John and his suffering fellow-Christians could have radiant spirits while suffering disappointment, loss, grief, and persecution under the harassments of Rome.

James S. Stewart was reminding us about the secret of that radiance when he wrote in *The Strong Name*:

> I am growing more and more convinced that a great part of the secret of achieving steadfastness and serenity in face of the battle of life is this—not only to commit your way to God in some high moment of conversion, but to do that very thing every morning, to go down on your knees and say, "Dear God, I do not ask to see the distant scene; but here, for the next twenty-four hours, is my life—I give it back to Thee, to guard, to bless, and control!"[1]

Stewart then added that this "will give the daily divine miracle its chance to work out in your experience, and will make all things as new and fresh and fair as when the morning stars sang together when the world was young."[2]

The world is no longer young, and we are all aging daily. Decay is at

1. James S. Stewart, *The Strong Name* (New York: Scribner's, 1941), p. 240.

2. Ibid.

work in all earthly things, ourselves included. It is a deca
prodding us to seek God's help while we pray and watch a
live for the final new order of things under God.

Meanwhile, we can go on serving. We can go on building relation
ships. We can go on blessing lives and being responsible. We can go
on obeying the mandates of our Master, open to God for renewal and
hope, and open to the people with whom life allows us contact. But
obedience is a must: actual and not merely intended, constant and not
spasmodic, no longer a mere duty but a living desire.

Full obedience to God is seldom convenient. John and the suffering
saints to whom he wrote the Revelation knew this all too well. But they
also knew that their obedience was keeping them on the side of the
future, that obedient living is investment living. They knew that labor
done in obedience is never a thing of the past. These labors maintain
our lives in cause-effect fashion, part of God's strategy to meet human
needs through human care. Like the true believers before us, we, too,
must stay sensitive to the moral order and remain steady within the
historical order, facing its appeals or constraints with trust in God. We
know that there is more to come. The best is yet to be! Meanwhile, we
must go on with our work while we watch for what God himself has
promised and will surely do.

A New Birth

Charles W. Eliot, of Harvard fame, was still alert and active in his
later years. A story appears in his biography by Henry James about a
visit the ninety-year-old man made to a home down the street from his
place. He went to see and hold a newborn child. As Eliot held the child
in his arms, he marveled out loud about the glory that surrounds new
life. Aware that he was nearing his own end, he said: "I wanted to hold
in my arms a life that was just beginning."[3]

A new birth puts us in touch with the promised meaning of life, a life
just beginning; and obedience to God keeps us moving toward that
promised new place which will be our true and final home. God has
planned it all, and he will fulfill that plan. Here again is the promise:
"Behold, I make all things new." Don't let anything in this world make
you miss it!

3. Henry James, *Charles W. Eliot: President of Harvard University, 1869–1909*, vol. 2 (Boston: Houghton Mifflin, 1930), p. 316.

14

The Bubble That Bursts

William (Billy) Franklin Graham

Vanity of vanities; all is vanity.

Ecclesiastes 1:2b (KJV)

Remember now thy Creator in the days of thy youth.

Ecclesiastes 12:1a (KJV)

People today are just as they were in Solomon's day, trying to find fun, amusement, pleasure, knowledge, security, love. It seems that almost all the young people I meet are on a quest of some sort.

Several years ago, a newspaper writer in a city where I was conducting a crusade wrote an article in which he reported that the youth of that city were saying they wanted more prosperity, more possessions. He went on to say that young people were trying to define themselves in terms of the clothes they wore, the things they bought, the places they went to. "But," he continued, "they are cynical, lonely, and in desperate need to return to the starting point, to discover who they are."

Are you like those young people, trying to discover who you are, where you came from, why you are here, where you are going, what is the purpose and meaning of life?

I've met so many entertainment stars whose day is past. How unhappy and lonely and empty they feel. I've talked with so many ath-

"The Man Who Had It All," by Billy Graham, © 1984 by Billy Graham Evangelistic Association. Used by permission.

letes whose day is past, and they feel the same way. So many former political leaders feel empty, lonely, forgotten. They have a moment of glamor, a moment when they're known, a moment when their name is on the front page; then it disappears.

Here in the Book of Ecclesiastes we have a picture of a man who had it all. It's as if Solomon told us, "I'm going to try every experience. I will seek every pleasure. I will gather the greatest wisdom. I will plumb every depth of living." Yet in spite of all this, he said, "Vanity of vanities; all is vanity." "It's all just a bubble that bursts," he declared. Though he had more material possessions than perhaps any other man in the history of the whole world, at the end of his life Solomon said, "Remember now thy Creator in the days of thy youth."

When Mark Chapman, at twenty-six, was sentenced for the murder of John Lennon, he said, "I'm standing on the edge of some crazy cliff." Like Solomon, his bubble had burst, and all he could feel was oblivion. How many young people feel like that? "I'm standing on the edge of some crazy cliff."

Solomon attained great knowledge. He wrote, "I . . . have gotten more wisdom than all they that have been before me in Jerusalem" (Eccles. 1:16, KJV). In 1 Kings we read that "Solomon's wisdom excelled the wisdom of all the children of the east country, all the wisdom of Egypt" (1 Kings 4:30, KJV). He said, "I gave my heart to know wisdom. . . . I perceived that this also is vexation of spirit. For in much wisdom is much grief" (Eccles. 1:17–18, KJV). "Vanity of vanities; all is vanity," he said. "It is a bubble that bursts."

Go ahead and get your Ph.D. I have men on my team with earned doctorates. But they will tell you that getting that diploma and having all the knowledge doesn't satisfy. You see, there's a difference between knowledge and wisdom. You can have your head full of knowledge, yet not have the wisdom to use the knowledge.

That's the trouble with the world today. We have allowed technology to outrun us, so that our morals have not caught up with our technology. Now we are in danger of destroying ourselves. With our stockpiles of knowledge, we have the knowledge of evil. We have discovered the key to our own genocide in the weapons we are creating.

Scripture has a lot to say about the mind. Jesus said that we are to love the Lord our God with all our heart, soul, strength, and mind (Luke 10:27). But you cannot come to Christ with your mind alone. Our natural minds have been affected by sin.

Even if you have all knowledge and all wisdom, you still cannot find

God with your mind. The Bible says, "The world by wisdom knew not God" (1 Cor. 1:21, KJV).

Scripture says, "Let this mind be in you, which was also in Christ Jesus" (Phil. 2:5, KJV). Do you have the mind of Christ? You can receive it now. The Bible says, "Be ye *transformed* by the renewing of your mind" (Rom. 12:2, KJV). Your mind is important, but you cannot think your way to God. You must come by faith, and then your mind will support your faith, as you study the Scriptures and prove them to be true.

Solomon had knowledge and wisdom. But they didn't satisfy. He said, "it's all vanity. It's a bubble that bursts."

Solomon gave himself to pleasure. In Ecclesiastes 2:1, he says, "I said in mine heart, 'Go to now, I will prove thee with mirth, therefore enjoy pleasure'" (KJV). So he tried wine, women, and song. He drank the finest wines from golden goblets (1 Kings 10:21). He had seven hundred wives and three hundred concubines (1 Kings 11:3). Talk about sex! He knew what sex was all about. He had every pleasure—everything at his beck and call. Hundreds of servants and every exotic food from around the world. He could afford every sensual pleasure that you can imagine. Yet he said, "It's all a bubble that bursts. It doesn't satisfy. It's all foolish. It's empty. All this pleasure has satisfied nothing in my soul. Only God can satisfy my soul."

Paul wrote to Timothy, "She that liveth in pleasure is dead while she liveth" (1 Tim. 5:6, KJV). You can have a lot of pleasures, but your soul be dead toward God.

We have traveled the world over to preach the gospel. We have traveled all over Africa. We have traveled all over Latin America. We have traveled all over Asia. We have traveled all over Europe. We have traveled all over the world to the islands of the sea. I have found one interesting fact. People are the same everywhere. You can go to a tribe among the Indians of Ecuador, and as far as spiritual things are concerned, those Indians are no different from an audience at Harvard University. The human heart is the same all over the world—longing for the same thing, searching for something that eludes us, and finding it only when we come to know Jesus Christ as our Lord and Savior. Permanent pleasure and happiness are not to be found anywhere else except in him.

Solomon also was the richest man in the history of the world. His wealth was staggering. His gold came by the ton (1 Kings 10:14). Imagine what a ton of gold would be worth at four hundred dollars per ounce. Solomon had many tons of it. He had a stable of forty thousand horses

(1 Kings 4:26). He sat on a throne of solid ivory inlaid with pure gold (1 Kings 10:18). His country home in the Forest of Lebanon was one of the most beautiful homes ever built (1 Kings 7:1–5).

Let me give you his daily grocery list. It is all recorded in the Bible: 185 bushels of fine flour, 375 bushels of meal, 10 fat oxen, 20 pasture-fed cattle, and 100 sheep and goats, besides deer and fowl (1 Kings 4:22–23). That was his grocery list for just one day. But one night he sat on the top of his home in Lebanon with indigestion. His hand clutched his empty heart. And he said, "Vanity of vanities; all is vanity." It's a bubble that bursts.

It's not wrong to be rich. It's not wrong to have money. It's not wrong to have a bank account, an insurance policy, a nice home. The important thing is your attitude toward money and material things. Are they first in your life? Jesus warned, "Beware of covetousness: for a man's life consisteth not in the abundance of the things which he possesseth" (Luke 12:15, KJV). Solomon could not find satisfaction in wealth. Nor will you.

Solomon had great power. No nation dared to defy him. He had more power than any other man in his generation. He had the greatest navy in the world. He looked upon his mighty military power and said, "This, too, has not satisfied."

How many people today are trying to climb to the top of the political heap in order to gain power and prestige! But when they get to the top, they discover these things don't satisfy either.

Solomon tried the aesthetic life. He said, "I made great works. I built great houses. I planted great vineyards. I made gardens and orchards. I planted trees. I made pools of water. I employed men singers and women singers, and the delights of men—many concubines. Whatever my eyes desired, whatever my heart desired, I got" (Eccles. 2:4–10).

Surely all those beautiful objects of art that he had, and those beautiful gardens that he built, and those musical recitals that he listened to, and those great shows that he put on must have brought the peace that he longed for. But they didn't. He said, "I looked on all the works that my hands had wrought, and on the labour that I had laboured to do: and, behold, all was vanity and vexation of spirit, and there was no profit under the sun" (Eccl. 2:11, KJV). "Vanity of vanities," he said. "It's a bubble that bursts. It doesn't satisfy. I haven't found my peace and happiness yet."

Solomon also turned to religion. He built the greatest temple the world has ever known. It took 183,300 men seven years to build Solomon's temple (1 Kings 5:13–16; 6:38). It was called one of the seven wonders of the world. His temple was an architectural triumph that could not be duplicated by the architects of our day. It was made of stone, granite, and marble so perfectly prepared at the quarries that neither hammer nor axe nor any tool of iron was heard in the house while it was being built (1 Kings 6:7). The whole temple—even the floor—was overlaid with pure gold (1 Kings 6:22, 30).

Solomon had religion. But God told the people of Judah through Isaiah the prophet, "Bring no more vain oblations; incense is an abomination unto me; the new moons and sabbaths, the calling of assemblies, I cannot away with; it is iniquity, even the solemn meeting" (Isa. 1:13, KJV). Religion itself had become iniquity in God's sight. It acted like a vaccination. When you are vaccinated against cholera, you may get sick the next day and feel like you have the flu. What you have is a little bit of cholera—just a little bit to keep you from getting the real thing when you travel in certain parts of the world.

Some of you have just enough religion to keep you from Christ. You do not know Christ for yourself. You are depending on your parents' religion, or you are depending on a church relationship, or you are depending on some religious exercise that you have gone through. But somehow deep in your heart you know that you are a long way from God and that sin is in your heart. Religion without a personal relationship with Christ will not save your soul or bring the peace that your soul longs for. Millions are searching for God through religion and not finding it.

Where is peace? Where is fulfillment? Where is happiness? Solomon said, "Fear God, and keep his commandments. . . . For God shall bring every work into judgment, with every secret thing, whether it be good, or whether it be evil" (Eccles. 12:13–14, KJV). He warns that a judgment is coming. Every secret thing that you have ever done, that you didn't think anybody knew about, will be revealed at that judgment. Solomon's experience and experiments led him back to God. He said, "Remember now thy Creator in the days of thy youth."

You need to find the real thing, the real pleasure, the real joy, the real satisfaction in Jesus Christ. In the twelfth chapter of Matthew we read, ". . . behold, a greater than Solomon is here" (v. 42, KJV). The one who is greater than Solomon in every area is the Lord Jesus Christ. Jesus said, "Ye shall know the truth, and the truth shall make you free" (John 8:32, KJV). He said, "I am the . . . truth" (John 14:6, KJV). Can you imagine anyone making a statement like that? "I am the embodiment of all truth. I am the truth. Come to me." All the things that you read about Solomon—all of his wisdom and knowledge—are found in their completeness and their perfection in Jesus Christ alone. The Scripture says, "In [Jesus Christ] are hid all the treasures of wisdom and knowledge" (Col. 2:3, KJV). You don't really have knowledge and wisdom until you come to know Christ.

The Bible says that when one person repents of sin, there is joy in heaven (Luke 15:7). Jesus can become the source of your joy. When you come to know Christ, the Holy Spirit produces joy in your heart, a joy that the world knows nothing about.

You can find wisdom, you can find joy, you can find pleasure, you can find riches. The Bible says of Christ, ". . . though he was rich, yet for your sakes he became poor, that ye through his poverty might be rich" (2 Cor. 8:9, KJV). Christ offers you riches beyond anything Solomon ever dreamed of—spiritual riches—glorious, lasting riches that you can lay up in the bank of heaven right now.

There is power in knowing Jesus Christ. Jesus said, "All power is given unto me in heaven and in earth" (Matt 28:18, KJV). All the power that is in all those stars and planets and all the power upon earth are his. And he offers it to you. There is a power and a boldness in Jesus Christ. That's the reason Paul could say, "I am not ashamed of the gospel of Christ: for it is the power [the dynamite] of God unto salvation to every one that believeth" (Rom. 1:16, KJV).

All the wisdom, all the joy, all the riches, all the greatness, all the power are in Christ. "Behold, a greater than Solomon is here" (Matt. 12:42, KJV). And he offers himself to you.

You ask, "But what do I have to do?" First, you must repent of your sins. You must say to God, "Lord, I have sinned." And you must be willing to turn from your sins—to change your value system and your way of living. Now that is the hard part. But when you are ready to do it, God will be there to help you. You cannot change yourself, but he will change you.

Second, you must come to Christ by faith. To have faith means "to commit," "to stand on," "to put your full weight upon." It means that you trust in Jesus Christ alone for salvation and forgiveness and fulfillment.

Third, you must promise to obey him, to follow him, to serve him. We forget that sometimes. You must promise that he will be your only Lord, your only Master. He will make the decisions in your life.

When you live that kind of life, you will have joy, happiness, and satisfaction. I'm asking you to trust Christ, to receive him. Come while you can. Tomorrow may be too late. There is no promise in the Bible about tomorrow. The Holy Spirit doesn't talk about tomorrow. The Bible says, ''Now is the accepted time . . . now is the day of salvation'' (2 Cor. 6:2, KJV). This your moment of decision. Don't put it off.

15

Let's Examine Our Prayer Life
Warren W. Wiersbe

> *For this cause I bow my knees unto the Father of our Lord Jesus Christ, Of whom the whole family in heaven and earth is named, That he would grant you, according to the riches of his glory, to be strengthened with might by his Spirit in the inner man; That Christ may dwell in your hearts by faith; that ye, being rooted and grounded in love, may be able to comprehend with all saints what is the breadth, and length, and depth, and height; And to know the love of Christ, which passeth knowledge, that ye might be filled with all the fulness of God. Now unto him that is able to do exceeding abundantly above all that we ask or think, according to the power that worketh in us, Unto him be glory in the church by Christ Jesus throughout all ages, world without end. Amen.*
>
> Ephesians 3:14–21 (KJV)

This prayer is one of the greatest prayers of all time. It was recorded by the apostle Paul when he was in prison and wrote his letter to the church at Ephesus.

Let's examine our own praying in the light of Paul's prayer. Let's take inventory of our prayer life. Why should we do this? Because everything in the Christian life rises or falls with prayer. God has ordained that prayer is the means by which we live the Christian life. If we don't pray, the Word of God becomes a dead book to us. If we don't pray, we don't have power to overcome temptation. If we neglect prayer, we are not able to witness or to work for the Lord. Prayer is the very heart of the Christian life.

I suspect that many of us need to examine our praying. The best way to do it, I think, is to use Paul's prayer as the example. We're going to ask ourselves four questions as we take inventory of our prayer life.

Question #1: Why Am I Praying?

In verse 14, Paul said, "For this cause I bow my knees unto the Father."

People have different motives for prayer. The Pharisees prayed that they might be heard and seen by men. People would hear them pray and say, "How spiritual they are!" I suppose that in our churches we have people who pray only for the praise of men. God doesn't answer that kind of prayer.

Some people pray simply out of habit. Praying is a good habit, but it shouldn't become a mere routine. Don't let your praying become an empty ritual that you go through without thinking.

Some people pray out of fear. Some people pray because of greed—they want certain things, and they ask God to provide them.

If I want to know what cause Paul was praying about, I have to go to the end of chapter 2, where he said, "[Ye] are [having been] built upon the foundation of the apostles and prophets, Jesus Christ himself being the chief corner stone; In whom all the building fitly framed together groweth unto an holy temple in the Lord: In whom ye also are builded together for an habitation of God through the Spirit" (Eph. 2:20–22, KJV). "For this cause I [Paul] bow my knees unto the Father. . . ."

Why was Paul praying? He *was praying because of his concern for the building of the church.* His motive for prayer was not to get things for Paul or to get things for the Ephesian believers. Paul's motive for prayer was the building of the church.

You and I need to realize that God is doing a great work in this world. We can't see all that is going on, and we will not see the finished product until the Lord Jesus returns and takes us to himself. God is building a temple—a spiritual temple—made up of living stones— people who have trusted Jesus Christ as their Savior.

Anything in my life that does not relate to the building of God's church is a waste of time, energy, and money. I fear that there are many individual Christians and many churches that are wasting time, energy, and money on projects that have no relationship to the building of the church.

When you and I pray, we never pray alone, because we are part of God's great building program. God is building a spiritual temple, the church, and my praying must relate to what God is doing. God's will in this world is that people be saved—made a part of this temple. He is calling out a people for his name.

If our prayers do not relate to what God is doing, our prayers will not be answered. Or if they *are* answered, we will regret it. The Scriptures say concerning Israel that God "gave them their request; but sent leanness into their soul" (Ps. 106:15, KJV). I have lived long enough to be thankful for unanswered prayer. I have talked to God about things that I thought were so important, and God said, "Those things do not relate to the work of the building of the church." So when you pray, you never pray alone—you are part of God's great building program going on in this world.

I have no right to ask God for anything that will not help in accomplishing his work. I have no right to ask God for anything that will help me but hurt you. If it hurts you, it hurts the church, and ultimately it will not help me. This is why in the Lord's Prayer there are no singular pronouns. It doesn't say "*my* Father," it says "*our* Father." It doesn't say "*my* daily bread," it says "*our* daily bread." "Forgive *us* our debts" (Matt. 6:9, 11, 12).

Do you see the greatness of this? When you pray in your room, you are not alone. God is with you, and you are part of a great worldwide family, the great temple that God is building. Just be sure that, when you pray, you are praying for God's glory, for the accomplishment of God's purposes, and not for your own selfish desires.

So our first question is simply, "Why am I praying?" Am I praying just to pray? Is it just a routine I go through? Am I praying to get some selfish thing that I want? Or am I praying because I need something to help God build his church? If you and I will ask God for those things that relate to the building of the church, God will answer.

Question #2: How Am I Praying?

It's possible to pray in the wrong attitude. Paul prayed as a son coming to a father. "I bow my knees unto the Father of our Lord Jesus

Christ." We come as children bowing before a Father, submitting to him.

It is interesting to study Paul's "spiritual posture" in Ephesians. It begins with the lost sinner dead in trespasses and sins (Eph. 2:1). When we trust Jesus Christ, we are made alive, and we are seated together with Christ in the heavenlies (Eph. 2:6). In chapter 4, we start to walk with Christ, and throughout chapters 4 and 5, the emphasis is on our walk. In chapter 6, we are told to stand for Christ. But between the "sitting" and the "walking" and the "standing" is the "bowing." The only way I can practice on earth my position in heaven is through prayer. My attitude in prayer ought to be that of a son coming to a father and submitting to his will.

The purpose of prayer is not to get our will done in heaven; the purpose of prayer is to get God's will done on earth. This is why we bow before the Father. Some people in the Bible stood when they prayed. Solomon stood and lifted up his hands to God when he prayed and dedicated the temple (2 Chron. 6:12). Abraham stood before the Lord and prayed for Sodom (Gen. 18:22). David went in and sat before the Lord (1 Chron. 17:16). I have a pastor friend who likes to walk up and down in his study, talking to God. I have enjoyed praying as I've walked down the busy streets of the city.

It's not the *physical* posture that Paul is talking about; he is talking about *spiritual* posture. Paul is saying, "Whether you are seated, whether you are standing, whether you are lying in a hospital bed, whether you are chained to a Roman soldier [as he was], it makes no difference. The *inward posture* of the soul is that of submission to the Father."

Prayer, you see, is a child's coming to the Father, not to tell the Father what to do, but to be available for the Father's will. Why am I praying? Well, it's for the purpose of the building up of the church. How am I praying? I'm praying as a child coming to the Father. Jesus said, "If ye then, being evil, know how to give good gifts unto your children, how much more shall your Father which is in heaven give good things to them that ask him?" (Matt. 7:11, KJV).

The beautiful part of the Christian life is pictured right here—bowing before the Father. This is the beginning of every blessing. We cannot work for God or walk with God, if we do not bow before him. We cannot fight the battles of life, we cannot accomplish the purposes of life, unless we are bowed before the Father.

What is your attitude in prayer? Are you fighting God? Some people say, "Jacob wrestled with the Lord." The Lord had to wrestle with Jacob and bring Jacob to a point of real surrender. There is no need to battle; there is no need to fight.

All we have to do is come to our loving Father and say, "Father, I have not come to overcome your reluctance; I have come to lay hold of your willingness. I am your child. I'm going to pray. I'm going to pray for the building up of your church. Don't give me anything that will not help in the building of your church. Father, I'm bowing before you in submission. I love you and thank you for the answers that you are going to give me as I pray."

Question #3: For What Am I Praying?

There are some basic requests that Paul makes. He prays for spiritual strength (v. 16), for spiritual depth (v. 17), for spiritual perspective (v. 18), and for spiritual fullness (v. 19).

Did you notice that Paul is praying about *spiritual* needs? So much of our praying focuses on the material and the physical. It is not unscriptural to pray about material and physical needs. In the Lord's Prayer, we are encouraged to ask for our daily bread. It is not wrong to pray for food and clothing. It is not wrong to pray about money to pay the bills. In my own life and ministry, I have seen God do wonderful things as we have prayed about material needs.

Nor is it wrong to pray about physical matters, such as healing. Paul did not neglect the outer man. I'm sure that when Paul spent a night and a day in the deep, he was praying about physical needs! I'm sure that when he experienced whippings, he was praying about those physical needs. He prayed for sick people who needed to be made well.

I have prayed about the physical needs of my own body and about the needs of others. As a pastor, I have many, many times been in sick rooms and hospital rooms, and we have prayed and asked God for strength for the body.

It is right to pray about material things, and it is right to pray about physical things, but these are not the greatest needs. Our greatest needs are spiritual.

What good is a healthy body if the inner man is not what it ought to be? What good is it to have money to spend on material goods if we don't know how to use them? If God gave me material blessings and physical blessings, but I was not spiritual enough to know how to use them, it would be a waste.

God is concerned about your body, but he is more concerned about the inner man that controls the body. The material and physical blessings of life must be matched by spiritual blessings. There must be Christian character. The inner man must be growing and becoming more like the Lord Jesus. Then God can trust us with the material and physical blessings of life.

Paul made several requests, and the first one is in verse 16, where he prayed for *spiritual strength*: "that he would grant you, according to the riches of his glory, to be strengthened with might by his Spirit in the inner man." There is in the believer an inner man that corresponds with the outer man. For example, my outer man needs food, otherwise I would die; and the inner man needs food, too. "Man shall not live by bread alone," said Jesus, "but by every word that proceedeth out of the mouth of God" (Matt. 4:41, KJV).

My outer man needs cleansing. If I didn't wash, I would pick up disease germs and get sick. The inner man needs cleansing as well. David prayed, ". . . wash me, and I shall be whiter than snow" (Ps. 51:7).

The outer man needs clothing for protection and for modesty, and the inner man needs clothing. In Colossians 3 Paul talked about dressing ourselves in the garments of grace.

The outer man needs exercise, otherwise we would get flabby; and the inner man needs exercise. Paul wrote to Timothy: "Exercise thyself . . . unto godliness" (1 Tim. 4:7, KJV).

Now the outer man needs strength, and the inner man needs strength. The Holy Spirit of God gives power to the inner man. I fear that too many Christians today are operating on "soul power," instead of Holy Spirit power. You see, you and I are spirit, soul, and body. Unsaved people operate on "soul power," the power of the mind, the emotions, and the will. Some people have more willpower than others. But we Christians have an added quality—the Holy Spirit living within.

When you were saved, the Holy Spirit of God came into your spirit, and the spirit of God bears witness with your spirit that you are God's child. If you don't have that inner witness, you have never been saved: ". . .if any man have not the Spirit of Christ, he is none of his" (Rom. 8:9, KJV).

The Holy Spirit of God wants to use your mind and heart and will in order to control your body. That's what Paul was praying about. He wanted these people to be strengthened with might in the inner man. Don't just operate on soul power—the intellect, the emotions, the will—because this will drain you. Let God fill you with his Holy Spirit.

Have you prayed like that lately, as you have faced the daily trials and demands of life? Do you say, "O God, strengthen me in the inner man"?

In verse 17, Paul prays for *spiritual depth*: "that Christ may dwell |that verb means "to settle down and feel at home"| in your hearts by faith; that ye, being rooted and ground in love. . . ." "Rooted" is an agricultural term. A tree has to send roots down deep to have stability and nourishment. "Grounded" is an architectural term. It refers to digging deep and laying a good foundation. All three of these pictures emphasize depth.

The great need today in our churches is for depth. We have shallow sentiment and shallow emotion that go on and off like the radio or the television set. We need depth! Have you prayed lately for spiritual depth? Have you prayed that Jesus Christ would get deeper and deeper into your life, that he would not just be a guest that you talk to occasionally, but that he would settle down and feel at home?

I wonder if there's anything in my life that makes the Lord Jesus not feel at home. I wonder if there is something in my inner man that grieves the Holy Spirit. Are you and I sending the roots of our faith down deep? Do we spend time in the Word of God, getting rooted there? Are we grounded? Are we building on a foundation that is deep and strong? Are we praying for spiritual strength and spiritual depth?

The third request is in verses 18 and 19. We must pray for *spiritual perspective*. We must ask God to help us comprehend and apprehend—get our hands on—"with all saints what is the breadth, and length, and depth, and height, And to know the love of Christ, which passeth knowledge. . . ."

That is a paradoxical statement, isn't it? How can you know something that passes knowledge? What Paul is saying is this: "The love of Christ is so vast and so wonderful and so great that we are going to spend all eternity getting to understand it. But let's start *now*."

Most of us, when we pray, pray about physical circumstances. We pray about the bills that have to be paid and about various material needs. When was the last time we prayed, "Dear God, open my eyes to see how great your love is"?

When God called Abraham, he told him to walk through the length and breadth of the land. Abraham lived in two dimensions. We live in four dimensions—the length and the breadth and the depth and the height! God's love is just so great and so vast that we need to pray for comprehension and perspective to enjoy it.

As I have traveled in various parts of the world, I have seen a great need. It is for the saints to love one another—"comprehend with all saints." Part of God's family is in heaven and part of God's family is on earth. One day all believers shall be in heaven with the Lord Jesus. Paul is telling me not to pray for narrowness, but for breadth. He wants me to get involved in the greatness of the love of God. We need this today.

God calls us to fullness, but sin creates emptiness. People who live in sin are empty people—they are drinking at the shallow, dirty cisterns of this world. Those who are Christians, who walk with God, have this artesian well of the water of everlasting life flowing within. This means fullness. Have you prayed lately for fullness?

Let me tell you how important fullness is. If my heart is not filled unto the fullness of God, something else is going to fill it. In the Bible, "filling" means "controlling." To be filled with anger means to be controlled by anger. Filled unto the fullness of God means to be controlled by God. Whatever fills you controls you.

I have friends who are "filled" with sports. They think athletics, they watch it on TV and listen to it on the radio, and they go to the games. They are controlled by sports. You and I as Christians should be controlled by Jesus Christ.

Paul said, "For to me to live is Christ" (Phil. 1:21, KJV). Christ is the One who makes life worth living, and he is the One who is living his life in us. Have you prayed lately, "O God, fill me unto the fullness of God. May my mind be filled with the thoughts of God. May my heart be filled with the love of God. May my will be filled with the power of God. May my life be disciplined, filled unto the fullness of God"?

When you put these four requests together, you can understand why Paul was such a great man. Imagine what would happen to our lives if daily we made these requests: "O God, strengthen me with might in the inner man by your Holy Spirit. Help me to go deeper today. Deliver me from a shallow experience that comes and goes. Give me a deep experience that is lasting. O Lord, deliver me today from narrowness and selfishness. Help me to comprehend the greatness of your love, and may I share this love with your whole family. Father, fill me unto the fullness of God."

Question #4: Am I Willing to Be Part of the Answer?

We have asked three questions: W*hy am I praying*? For the building up of the church. H*ow am I praying*? As a child bowed before my Father. F*or what am I praying*? For spiritual strength, depth, perspective, and fullness. Are you ready for the question that really hits you between the eyes? In verse 20 Paul asks this: Are you willing to be part of the answer? "Now unto him that is able to do exceeding abundantly above all that we ask or think, according to the power that worketh in us."

Do you know what Paul is saying here? Paul is saying that I must be willing to be a part of the answer. It took me so long to learn this. The greatest blessing in life is not to *get* an answer to prayer, it is to *be* an answer to prayer. The greatest thing that could happen to you today would not be to get an answer to prayer. The greatest thing that could happen to you today would be for the power of God to work in your life so that you would go out and be an answer to prayer.

You can illustrate this from the Bible. Take Moses, for example. Moses had fled Egypt. For forty years he cared for his father-in-law's flocks out in the desert. God was dealing with him. I am sure that Moses prayed for his people down in Egypt. Exodus 3 records that one day Moses met God at the burning bush, and God said, "I've heard the cries of my people [and that included Moses]. I am come down to deliver my people."

Then God said, "Moses, I'm going to send *you*." Now that's a different story, isn't it? "Moses, are you willing to be part of the answer?" At first, Moses was not willing; and God humbled him and brought him to the place of submission. Are you willing to be part of the answer?

Consider Nehemiah, a man I greatly admire. One day Nehemiah met his brother, who had just come back from a trip to Jerusalem. Nehemiah asked his brother, "How are things in Jerusalem?" His brother said, "Terrible! The walls are down, the gates are burned, the people are living in humiliation. The Gentiles are mocking them." Nehemiah began to pray. In the first chapter of Nehemiah, you find him praying to God for the city of his fathers. And God said, "Nehemiah, I have heard your prayer. I am going to send you!" Nehemiah didn't just *get* an answer to prayer; he *became* an answer to prayer.

It's interesting to note that Jesus said to his disciples, "Pray ye therefore the Lord of the harvest, that he will send forth labourers . . ." (Matt. 9:38, KJV). In the very next chapter, Jesus sent them out! This is why it is important to be careful what you pray about. You may be praying to-day, "O God, our missionaries need money; they need help. There is a need for workers." Be careful now! Are you willing to be a part of the answer? I have come to the conclusion that unless I am willing to be a part of the answer, I have no right to pray. My first prayer ought to be, "O God, make me willing to be a part of the answer." God doesn't want only to answer prayer *for* you. He wants to answer prayer *in* you and *through* you. He wants you to be an answer to prayer.

One of the greatest blessings in life is to have someone look at you and say, "You met my need today. God made you an answer to prayer." If you and I are willing to be part of the answer, then Ephesians 3:21 will take place: "Unto him be glory in the church. . . ." That's why we're praying to begin with—for the building up of the church! "Unto him be glory in the church by Christ Jesus throughout all ages." It will last for-ever!

When God answers prayer in and through your life, that answer is going to last forever and glorify God. A million years from now, God will still get glory because you were willing to be a part of the answer.

Why are you praying? How are you praying? For what are you pray-ing? Are you willing today to be part of the answer?

May this prayer inventory stir us up to pray as we ought!

16

Is It Well with Your Family?

W. *Graham Smith*

".. . Is it well with you? Is it well with your husband? Is it well with the child?"

2 Kings 4:26

Every time I think of Mother's Day, I see roses! As a small boy, growing up in Canada, I remember how everyone wore a rose on Mother's Day—a red rose if your mother was still alive, a white one if she had died. I can still see my father entering his pulpit, proudly wearing his red rose. His words still re-echo in the chambers of memory, as he spoke with affection and gratitude about his beloved mother and the godly influence she had exerted on his life.

I know that we should love and honor our mothers every day of the year. Yet how appropriate that on one beautiful Lord's Day each springtime, we should afford them that special honor and recognition they so richly deserve. It is a fitting occasion also to reflect on family life in general and the place the family enjoys in God's eternal purpose for his children. The Psalmist reminds us that "God sets the lonely in families" (Psalm. 68:6, KJV).

One of the towering figures in Old Testament history is that fearless prophet of the Lord, Elisha. As he traversed the length and breadth of the land of Israel proclaiming the Word of God, it was his custom periodically to visit Shunem, a village in the central area of the country. A woman of considerable wealth lived here with her husband, who farmed a portion of land on the outskirts of the village. This devout

127

couple soon came to hold Elisha in such high esteem that they actually built onto their home an additional room that was reserved for the use of the prophet when he passed that way.

After a time, Elisha asked his servant what could be done to recompense these good, kind people for their friendship and hospitality. Since, in the inscrutable providence of God no child had been born to them, Elisha finally decided to call the woman to him and announce to her that her oft-repeated prayer would be answered, her fondest wish fulfilled. In the mercy of God she would bear a son. One year later she did.

Needless to say, the little fellow was his parents' pride and joy. He grew to be sturdy and strong. But one terrible day, during harvesttime, he slipped out of the house, made his way bareheaded to the field where his father and his helpers were harvesting the grain, and there was stricken with deadly sunstroke. They carried him home to his mother, and an hour or two later, as she held him in her arms, he died. Demented with grief, this godly woman turned instinctively in her hour of need to the prophet. She saddled a donkey and hastened to Carmel, twenty-five miles away, where Elisha maintained his headquarters. As she drew near, the prophet saw and recognized her from a distance. Summoning his servant Gehazi, he said to him, "Run at once to meet her, and say to her, 'Is it well with you? Is it well with your husband? Is it well with the child?' "

Is It Well with You?

"Is it well with you?" There is no greater privilege and responsibility bestowed by God upon anyone than that of being a wife and mother. No one has a more profound and enduring influence upon those around her than the mother in a home, whether she realizes it or not. William Ross Wallace gave vivid expression to this truth when he wrote: "The hand that rocks the cradle/Is the hand that rules the world."

In 1948, when Dr. Harry Emerson Fosdick retired as minister of Riverside Church in New York City, he paid an eloquent tribute to his wife. He had been puzzled all his life, he said, by the fact that, on the whole, women have not accomplished as much in a public way as men have accomplished. Why is this so? Obviously, the brains of women are as good as or perhaps better than the brains of men. Yet the sober truth is that there have been relatively few women in the list of composers, artists, scientists, and statesmen. "At last," said Dr. Fosdick, "I know the answer. No woman ever had a wife!"

Because of the abiding influence of the wife and mother in the home, how imperative it is that she be a dedicated, consistent Christian.

Lord Byron, the English poet, had a mother who virtually despised him because he suffered from a congential lameness. She occasionally even taunted him about his physical handicap. Inevitably, he grew up to be a frustrated, disillusioned, cynical profligate, who renounced his home and sought his pleasure where he could find it. At thirty-five years of age and dying, far from his homeland, he wrote:

> My days are in the yellow leaf,
> The flowers and fruits of love are gone;
> The worm, the canker, and the grief
> Are mine alone.

Contrast Byron's mother with Susannah Wesley, who bore seventeen children. She made time each week to take each of those boys and girls aside and counsel with them and speak to them about the love of Jesus. Is it any wonder that one boy in that family became the greatest preacher of his generation, and another son the greatest hymn-writer in the English language? With a mother like that, we can understand why Charles Wesley wrote these lines, ardent with devotion to Christ:

> O for a thousand tongues to sing
> My great Redeemer's praise,
> The glories of my God and King,
> The triumphs of His grace!
>
> Jesus! The Name that charms our fears,
> That bids our sorrows cease;
> 'Tis music in the sinner's ears;
> 'Tis life and health and peace.

Happily, parents are beginning to realize that a mother's finest place is in the home. Let no homemaking wife and mother ever consider herself a "second-class citizen". Financial stringency makes it almost obligatory for some mothers to work, but no one can deny that the income of many women is used almost exclusively to provide luxury items that could very well be done without.

I know many homes where it must be a real effort to make ends meet, yet the mother is there when the children come home from school and the husband comes home from the office. Her spirit pervades the home. She makes time to pray for her children, to teach them obedience, courtesy, good manners, and consideration for others. In the words of the Book of Proverbs: ". . . She is worth far more than rubies. . . . Her children arise and call her blessed; her husband also, and he praises her" (Prov. 31:10, 28, KJV).

A minister and his wife, whom I knew well, had one son. When he was a little boy, his mother was so wrapped up in church work and in her bridge club and in a dozen other community projects that the poor child was not *brought* up—he was *dragged* up. Ladies in the congregation darned the holes in the elbows of his sweaters. His mother was too busy. But she lived to reap the bitter fruit of her failure. The boy grew up to be irresponsible and dissolute. For the past thirty years, he has been officially "missing"; no one knows whether he is living or dead.

Lord Shaftesbury, that great Christian statesman and social reformer of the nineteenth century, once exclaimed, "Give me a generation of Christian mothers, and I will change the face of English society in twelve months."

In the second chapter of Exodus, we have one of the great dramatic passages of the Bible. The Egyptian princess has discovered baby Moses floating in his basket amongst the bulrushes of the River Nile and decides to adopt him. Miriam, Moses' sister, comes forward and tells the princess that she knows a woman who would be an ideal nurse for the child. All unknown to the princess, Miriam brings the baby's own mother to care for him. Listen to what the princess said to the mother of Moses: "Take this child away, and nurse him for me, and I will give you your wages" (Exod. 2:9).

God says that to every mother still. Our children do not belong to us at all; they belong to God. "Take this child," he says, "and nurse it for me, and I will give you your wages." Remember, Christian mother, God always pays good wages. If you are faithful to the sacred trust committed to you, you will indeed lay up for yourself treasure in heaven.

Is It Well with Your Husband?

"Is it well with your husband?" Is he a Christian? Is he accepting responsibility for the spiritual welfare of the home?

Did you notice what this father did in our story? He did a shameful and despicable thing. The little boy toddled out to the field. His father didn't even notice that the child was bareheaded, with the fierce sun beating down upon him. He was too busy to notice. And when the child was stricken, did the father carry him into the shade of a tree and sprinkle water on his face? Did he bend over him and seek to revive him? Did he pick him up in his strong arms and hurry back home with him? No! He was too busy. The crops had to be harvested before the rains came. He simply said to one of his servants, "Carry him to his mother" (2 Kings 4:19). The wretched man shirked his responsibility toward his child. He asked someone else to do for his child the very thing he should most certainly have done himself.

Many fathers do precisely the same thing today. They are so busy at the office, in the club or lodge, in the garden or in the church, that they haven't time, they say, to keep the promise they made before God when their child was dedicated, namely, "to bring him up in the nurture and admonition of the Lord." "Carry him to his mother"—"carry him to the minister"—"carry him to the Sunday-school teacher"—"carry him to the scoutmaster"—"carry him to the summer youth conference."

The father's place is in the home, just as the mother's place is there. Of course, he cannot always be there, but he should be there whenever he can. It is tragic for a man to give so much time and energy to his public work that his wife and children seldom see him, and, further, that the bits of time he gives them are spoiled by his being tired and easily irritated. It is hard for a father to know how deeply little children want their father's undivided time and attention. That is why we should give them "prime time," "quality time." It certainly is not fair for children always to have to compete with the newspaper or the TV. Let me tell you fathers today that if you are shirking your responsibility to your children, you will live to regret it bitterly.

The Bible says that the father is the head of the household (Eph. 5:23). This does not mean that he is to be a bossy tyrant, but it does mean that he is responsible before God for the welfare of the family: financially, educationally, spiritually. Unfortunately, in recent years the notion that the father is just another fellow around the house, almost wholly devoid of honorable status and not even primarily responsible for the financial support of the family, has won popular acceptance. The results of this heresy are pathetic to behold.

The Protestant Reformers spoke and wrote much about "the priesthood of all believers," and about the father being a priest in his own household. The function of a priest, as you know, is to lead people to God. Did you realize that for the first 250 years of Protestantism there were no Sunday schools as we know them today? The Reformation was completed by 1530, but the first Sunday school was founded in 1780 in Gloucester, England, by Robert Raikes, who had a deep concern for the children in the slums of the city who were receiving no instruction in the gospel. Was the spiritual training of children neglected during those 250 years? Of course not. In that period parents took seriously the Christian education of their children. They were unwilling to entrust that solemn task to anyone else. They regarded it as their responsibility before God.

Still today all Christian fathers and mothers have the divinely imposed responsibility of leading their family to the feet of God. A truly Christian home is one in which parents are role models of genuine Christian living, where they instruct their children in the things of the Lord, where family devotions are an integral part of daily family life, and where they show the children that God is the most important reality in anyone's life. After all, why should I as a parent expect anyone else, even a dedicated Sunday-school teacher, to introduce my child to Jesus Christ and to the treasures of the Scriptures? That is my responsibility, and how great are the rewards if I am faithful in the discharge of my duty!

J. Wilbur Chapman, perhaps the finest evangelist the Presbyterian Church in the U.S.A. has known, once used the following illustration in a sermon. He said that he had just heard of a father who came into the bedroom where his young son lay dying. The boy had been ill for so long that his body was badly wasted, and it was painful for him even to lie on the bed. As the father entered, the lad said, "Daddy, lift me up for a moment."

The father put his hands under the emaciated body and raised his son just a little off the bed. "Lift me higher," he said; "Daddy, lift me higher." The father lifted him up until he held him above his head. When he took him down, the boy was dead. It would seem as if that father had actually lifted his son into the very arms of Christ. When Dr. Chapman had concluded the service, a man with tears in his eyes came up to him and said, "Dr. Chapman, it happened just as you said. I went into his room, and my minister was with me. I lifted him up, and his weak voice came back to me in whispers, saying, 'Higher, Daddy, higher." When I took him down, he had gone. But, sir, I had lifted him into the arms of Christ long before, for when he was a very small boy I taught him of a Savior's love, and told him what it means to be a Christian."

This is the work that every father is called upon to do. If you are a father, you are called to do it. You cannot excuse yourself from it, nor can you delegate it entirely to others. It is your responsibility.

Is It Well with the Child?

"Is it well with the child?" If it is well with the father and the mother, it will certainly be well with the children, for God has promised, "Train up a child in the way he should go, and when he is old he will not depart from it" (Prov. 22:6).

Of course, if you think more about your children's intellectual attainments and their material prosperity than you do about their relationship to Jesus Christ, you can't expect much from them. Many parents are far more excited about getting their children into a first-rate college than they are concerned about their children's eternal salvation. "Education" is a far more important word in many people's vocabulary than the word "salvation." I'm not making a snide remark about education when I say that. God knows, we can't get too much education. But what I am saying is that we should regard everything that this world has to offer in the light of eternity. Looking at things in true perspective, this world, our present life, is but a preparatory class for eternity. One hundred years from today, you will be somewhere. One thousand years—a million years—from today, you and your children will be somewhere. Increase the multiple and you only increase the truth: no one is ever really prepared to face this world until he is prepared for the world that is to come.

Do you pray *for* your children and *with* them, too? Can you honestly say that you are doing all you possibly can to guide them along the road that leads to life eternal? If not, then no matter what else you may accomplish, in God's sight you are a pathetic failure.

> O happy home, where Thou art loved the dearest,
> Thou loving Friend, and Saviour of our race,
> And where among the guests there never cometh
> One who can hold such high and honored place!

O happy home, whose little ones are given
Early to Thee, in humble faith and prayer,
To Thee, their Friend, who from the heights of heaven
Dost guide and guard with more than mother's care!

Oh happy home, where Thou art not forgotten
When joy is overflowing, full and free;
O happy home, where every wounded spirit
Is brought, Physician, Comforter, to Thee,

Until at last, when earthly toil is ended,
All meet Thee in the blessed home above,
From whence Thou camest, where Thou hast ascended,
Thy everlasting home of peace and love!

17

God's Word to Fathers
Lane G. Adams

"Honor your father and mother, that your days may be long in the land which the LORD *your God gives you."*

Exodus 20:12

Be subject to one another out of reverence for Christ. Wives, be subject to your husbands, as to the Lord. For the husband is the head of the wife as Christ is the head of the church, his body, and is himself its Savior. As the church is subject to Christ, so let wives also be subject in everything to their husbands. Husbands, love your wives, as Christ loved the church and gave himself up for her, that he might sanctify her, having cleansed her by the washing of water with the word, that he might present the church to himself in splendor, without spot or wrinkle or any such thing, that she might be holy and without blemish. Even so husbands should love their wives as their own bodies. He who loves his wife loves himself. For no man ever hates his own flesh, but nourishes and cherishes it, as Christ does the church, because we are members of his body. "For this reason a man shall leave his father and mother and be joined to his wife, and the two shall become one flesh." This mystery is a profound one, and I am saying that it refers to Christ and the church; however, let each one of you love his wife as himself, and let the wife see that she respects her husband.

Children, obey your parents in the Lord, for this is right. "Honor your father and mother" (this is the first commandment with a promise), "that it may be well with you and that you may live long on the earth." Fathers, do not provoke your children to anger, but bring them up in the discipline and instruction of the Lord.

Ephesians 5:21–6:4

Some time back I heard a story about a man who received his doctor's degree in psychology with highest honors. The honors

135

were awarded because in his dissertation he had reduced all child-rearing to three simple principles. Ten years later he had three children and no principles.

Most of us have felt that way about being parents. I certainly have felt that way about being a father. Theory is often stoned to death by the brutal facts of reality.

Part of the reason for this confusion is the raging conflict of opinion about what constitutes good parenting. Which expert are you going to believe? Is it too simple to ask the counsel of the One who invented the idea of man and woman, created them, thus constituting the first family, and then gave them children? What word does God give us in regard to this matter?

I've heard dozens of sermons on the home and delivered a few myself as well, but I've never heard of anyone selecting this verse in Exodus 20:12 for a sermon on this subject. Exodus 20, of course, is the chapter that tells of the great event of God's giving his law to Moses on Mount Sinai. It tells us in detail what the Ten Commandments are.

In his summary of the Ten Commandments in Matthew 22:37–40, our Lord Jesus Christ separated them into two tables. He said, "You shall love the Lord your God with all your heart, and with all your soul, and with all your mind. . . . And . . . you shall love your neighbor as yourself." The first four commandments have to do with love for God, and the last six have to do with love for neighbor. The first four establish the authority of God. What follows stuns me. *God transfers his authority from himself to the father and the mother in the home*. There is no mention of the state as recipient of his authority, nor is there any mention of the church.

This fact seems tremendously significant to me because it makes the home the most important institution on the face of the earth. It thereby exalts the roles of father and mother, husband and wife, above every other position in society. To be the recipients of God's authority is an awesome responsibility. Yet, at the same time it is an exalted responsibility.

Studies have shown that a destabilized home inevitably destabilizes every other institution in society, including the state. It is beyond contradiction that the future character of any nation is dependent upon the quality of the children that are produced for succeeding generations. The old saying "The hand that rocks the cradle rules the world" is given a great deal of reinforcement at this point. The family is the essential building block of all of society. What happens there will either stabilize or destabilize everything else in society. It seems to me, then, that the job we do as fathers and mothers and husbands and wives is the most important work we do on this earth.

Very honestly, as I have examined the implications of this fact, I have become appalled at the offhand way that I approached both marriage and fatherhood. I had no training nor preparation for these responsibilities, nor was any ever offered to me.

Even today little real preparation is offered to those venturing into marriage and parenthood. We move heaven and earth to prepare people for vocation and profession, but, at best, we offer a few hours of inadequate counseling for the most important work they are ever apt to do.

People who reach the pinnacle of success in the business, professional, or political world, yet fail in the home, seem to have a hollow victory. Professional success—but personal failure. I remember hearing a prominent pastor say that it occurred to him once as he drove into his driveway after a particularly hard day at the office, that he was about to begin the most important work of his entire day—his handling of his relationships with his wife and children. Think about that!

The Ten Commandments reveal the character and will of God to man. In the midst of that revelation is his evaluation of the home. This surely means that the home is the most important educational institution on the face of this earth; and those who hold the responsible roles in the home bear, at one and the same time, exalted honor from God and awesome responsibility to each other and to their children.

Since this is Father's Day, let's examine some of the responsibilities of the father in the home. In the New Testament is found a most helpful passage in Ephesians 5:21 through 6:24. Time does not permit an exhaustive exposition of this text, so permit me to summarize. The husband is to teach his children to honor their mother by honoring her himself in his own relationship with her. He is to model how honor behaves in relation to her. He is to love his wife as Christ loved the church and died for it. By precept and example, he is to lead her into holiness and mutual righteous living through the Word of God. Indeed, he is to love his wife as he loves his own body. He is to cherish and protect his wife and to assume responsibility for providing both for her needs and for those of the children. I believe that the protection he is to give goes beyond the merely physical. He is to protect her spiritually, emotionally, and psychologically. Surely this fleshes itself out in encouragement and affirmation, but especially in listening carefully to his wife, responding to her, and, as verse twenty-one suggests, being willing to yield to her wisdom when it is obviously better than his own.

It is interesting that at the beginning of Ephesians 6 that marvelous home-honoring fifth commandment is applied to children, but then the further responsibility of the father is spelled out in these words: "Fathers, do not exasperate your children; instead [fathers], bring them up in the training and instruction of the Lord" (v. 4, NIV). In a society where men have foisted their spiritual and educational responsibilities either on their wives or on a remote school, this exhortation is indeed enlightening. It is the father who is responsible for the spiritual, educational, emotional, and psychological well-being of his children. This is not to say that his wife doesn't share this staggering responsibility, for he certainly cannot do it alone. But he is the one who will finally answer to God for the job done.

While the father is carefully warned in this passage against exasperating his children, in Colossians 3:21 he is cautioned not to embitter them, or they will become discouraged. The way to avoid these problems is really quite simple. Just make sure that you give as many affirmations and encouragements and compliments as you do corrections. You will do better still if you are more generous with positive affirmations than with corrections.

Most important of all, remember that there is nothing a father can substitute for time spent with his children. I don't mean just being in their general vicinity, but holding direct contact and conversation with them. All of us, this preacher included, are too busy succeeding at things of lesser importance than this job that God has given to us. Back in the sixties and early seventies there was a popular song entitled, "The Cat's in the Cradle." How curious that it should have come out of the era of the worst youth rebellion America has ever seen. The point it makes needs no comment.

> My child arrived just the other day;
> He came to the world in the usual way.
> But there were planes to catch and bills to pay;
> He learned to walk while I was away.
> And he was talkin' 'fore I knew it,

And as he grew he'd say,
"I'm gonna be like you, Dad,
You know I'm gonna be like you."
And the cat's in the cradle and the silver spoon,
Little boy blue and the man in the moon.
"When you comin' home, Dad?"
"I don't know when, but we'll get together then;
You know we'll have a good time then."

My son turned ten just the other day;
He said, "Thanks for the ball, Dad, come on let's play.
Can you teach me to throw?"
I said, "Not today, I got a lot to do."
He said, "That's okay."
And he walked away, but his smile never dimmed,
It said, "I'm gonna be like him,
Yeah, you know I'm gonna be like him."
And the cat's in the cradle and the silver spoon,
Little boy blue and the man in the moon.
"When you comin' home, Dad?"
"I don't know when, but we'll get together then;
You know we'll have a good time then."

Well, he came home from college just the other day;
So much like a man I just had to say,
"Son, I'm proud of you, can you sit for awhile?"
He shook his head and he said with a smile,
"What I'd really like, Dad, is to borrow the car keys;
See you later, can I have them please?"
And the cat's in the cradle and the silver spoon,
Little boy blue and the man in the moon.
"When you comin' home, Son?"
"I don't know when, but we'll get together then;
You know we'll have a good time then."

I've long since retired, my son's moved away;
I called him up just the other day.
I said, "I'd like to see you, if you don't mind."
He said, "I'd love to, Dad, if I can find the time.
You see, my new job's a hassle and the kids have the flu,
But it's sure nice talkin' to you."
And as I hung up the phone, it occurred to me,
He'd grown up just like me;
My boy was just like me.

And the cat's in the cradle and the silver spoon,
Little boy blue and the man in the moon.
"When you comin' home, Son?"
"I don't know when, but we'll get together then;
Dad, we're gonna have a good time then."

Harry Chapin, "The Cat's in the Cradle"
© 1974 Story Songs Ltd.
Used with permission.

Although I've read that song many times, it still puts a lump in my throat and a pang of regret in my heart that I did not spend more quality time with our Susie when she was growing up. And how quickly they do grow up. Surely, you won't make that mistake!

About now the average father is ready to throw up his hands in horror, shouting, "What you ask is impossible!"

Humanly, it is impossible. But with God all things are possible. I assure you that only the Spirit who gave the law and raised Jesus from the dead could possibly enable us to accomplish this task. Only the Spirit who hovered over the waters of creation can re-create in us the mind and heart and will to do this kind of job as a father. But that is precisely what the promise of God is to those who put their faith in his Son Jesus Christ as their Lord and Savior. He promises that his Spirit will come to dwell within the very inmost citadel of their being in order to strengthen them in mind, heart, and will, that they may fulfill his Word on earth.

We must come to a point of initial and continual commitment to Jesus Christ to precipitate this indwelling by his Spirit. Half measures won't do.

We must also commit ourselves to a discipline. Our minds must be re-educated by daily study of the Word of God concerning all that he expects of us and all that is available to help us meet those expectations.

Moreover, we must hold intimate communion and conversation with our heavenly Father, if we are ever to reflect even dimly to our wives and children the perfect attributes of his fatherhood. We must dedicate ourselves to a continuing education in this most important task of human fatherhood, if we are ever to master it according to his will. Never in Christian history have so many excellent resources been available. I urge you to get everything you can that has been written and spoken by James Dobson from Focus on the Family. The writings of Allen Peterson, Howard Hendricks, and many others are also commendable.

I can assure you, speaking from the perspective of one with a slightly graying head, that I echo the words of the apostle John, "I have no greater joy than to hear that my children are walking in the truth" (3 John 4, NIV). Inexpert as my parenting was and far short of the ideal that I've spelled out for you, it is nevertheless my unspeakable joy to have seen our only child, Susie, set up her own home and become a marvelous mother of four. How much I thank God for her mother!

Children grow up so quickly. Give fatherhood your best, and give it right now:

> And the cat's in the cradle and the silver spoon,
> Little boy blue and the man in the moon.
> "When you comin' home, Son?"
> "I don't know when, but we'll get together then;
> Dad, we're gonna have a good time then."

18

The Chains at West Point
Richard P. Camp, Jr.

For the law of the Spirit of life in Christ Jesus has set me free from the law of sin and death.

Romans 8:2

Few places in the world have more significance for Independence Day than West Point.

Here, in 1775, General George Washington's emissaries selected a site to protect access to the Hudson River Valley from the British. Their best choice was "the West Point," where the river narrows into an s-shaped bend, surrounded by high cliffs, and where it is buffeted by unpredictable winds and difficult tides.

Here, in 1778, the colonists had one of the most strategic fortifications in the new nation. While Washington and his troops suffered through the winter at Valley Forge, Americans at West Point were using the unique terrain and river configuration to build a defensive position that would prevent the British from sailing up the Hudson. The British strategy was to use the Hudson River to cut off New England from the rest of the states.

Here, in 1778, a great chain was erected across the river from West Point to Constitution Island. The links, some of which are still on display at Trophy Point, were as large as dinner plates. Because of its weight, the chain had to be supported by log rafts. Its use as a deterrent apparently was successful—it was never tested.

And here, in 1780, Major General Benedict Arnold, hero of Saratoga and then commander of West Point and the Hudson Highlands, turned traitor and tried to sell the fortress to the British.

West Point today is dotted with monuments to the past. Cannons, chains, statues, and restored fortifications remind us of the struggle for freedom. Monuments to fighting men and renowned battles hold up the historic role of this place in the first two centuries of our nation's history. These monuments exist not only to point to the past but to help preserve the future. They say to us, "Freedom is not free!" They stand to remind future generations that freedom is not free. From Valley Forge to Normandy, from Gettysburg to the Philippines, from West Point to Inchon, freedom has never been free!

On this Independence Sunday, we enjoy the fruit of a great heritage. Our parades and picnics should serve as colorful reminders that freedom has come at great price. Yet millions of Americans enjoy these benefits without regard for the foundations from which they come. It is important to note that for the colonists and the framers of our Declaration of Independence, freedom was an everyday vocation. It was part of a spiritual movement.

Our heritage as Americans must be seen that way. Many of those early leaders didn't attend church regularly. Some, like Thomas Jefferson, were Deists. But they had in their minds and hearts a deep dedication to God. They were convinced that liberty and equality were given by God in his creative wisdom. "We hold these truths to be self-evident," they wrote in the immortal lines of the Declaration of Independence, "that all men are created equal, that they are endowed by their Creator with certain unalienable Rights, that among these are Life, Liberty and the pursuit of Happiness."

The founders of our nation believed that they would be free men so long as they lived in obedience to the authority of God. That truth has not changed! Freedom is still a spiritual movement; freedom under God is its foundation. To be able to think, believe, and act from a conscience in subservience to the will of God is the greatest freedom of all. Written by the Reverend Samuel Smith, and first sung in historic Park Street Church on Boston Common on July 4, 1832, the following song, familiar to us all, expresses the role of freedom in its American context.

My country, 'tis of thee,
Sweet land of liberty,
Of thee I sing;

Land where my fathers died,
Land of the pilgrims' pride,
From every mountain-side
   Let freedom ring.

My native country, thee,
Land of the noble free,
   Thy name I love;
I love thy rocks and rills,
Thy woods and templed hills;
My heart with rapture thrills
   Like that above.

The final stanza of this hymn is sung in the Cadet Chapel of West Point each Sunday at the conclusion of the service.

Our fathers' God, to thee,
Author of liberty,
   To thee we sing;
Long may our land be bright
With freedom's holy light;
Protect us by thy might,
   Great God, our King.

But this freedom, this freedom under God, is not free. Edmund Burke once said, "All it takes for evil to prosper is for good men to do nothing." In other words, unless good people pay the price of responsible leadership, the unprincipled and the unscrupulous will dominate.

Many of the perils that threaten our heritage of freedom as a nation are reflections of the struggles that go on within us as individuals. Rebellion, fear, futility, and oppression are enemies of free people—shackles to both political liberty and spiritual freedom. A long time ago the apostle Paul wrote, "Plant your feet firmly therefore within the freedom that Christ has won for us, and do not let yourselves be caught again in the shackles of slavery" (Gal. 5:1, *Phillips*). Paul was not referring to any particular nation, and it would be dangerous for us to make that application to America or any other country. He was speaking, however, to Christians who had the possibility of being shackled by a system. For those first-century Christians living in Galatia, it was the system of Jewish legalism. Today, followers of Christ confront a different but equally enslaving system composed of the values and forces at work in our neo-pagan society that produce rebellion and fear and futility and oppression.

The good news today is that God has put into effect a power that delivers us from the shackles of any such system. Saint Paul describes this power in chapter eight of his letter to the Romans. You can experience the freedom of which he writes by applying the following principles in his argument to your own life:

1. *At the root of the system is rebellion against God.* Its most common manifestation is indifference toward God. The basis of our inability to handle the system lies in what the apostle calls "the law of sin and death," which produces fear, futility, and oppression. To counter this rebellion, God has placed in motion a powerful force called "the Spirit of life in Christ Jesus." Where God the Holy Spirit is in control, the old chains are compelled to give way. The old chains are broken. Just as the law of gravity is overcome by a stronger opposing force, so we are set free from the law of sin and death by the law of life in Christ.

Some of our West Point cadets have earned their airborne wings and know what it is to jump out of an airplane and feel the power of gravity as you plummet to the earth. Your parachute serves as a mediating factor, but the law of gravity prevails. If you are in a hot-air balloon, however, and the air is heated so that it becomes lighter than the atmospheric air, you counter the law of gravity as you ascend into the sky. In the same way, the law of the Spirit of life in Christ delivers us from the law of sin and death. But our freedom is not free! The law of the Spirit takes effect only as we trust Christ as our Savior and then follow him each day.

2. *The system produces fear.* Little children are usually afraid of the dark. As they grow, they acquire adult fears, such as fear of an uncertain future or of failure or of death or even of the system itself. But the good news is that we "did not receive a spirit that makes [us] . . . slave[s] again to fear, but [we] received the Spirit of sonship. And by him we cry, 'Abba, Father'" (Rom. 8:15, NIV).

A little child may be reluctant to go out into the dark night alone, but holding Daddy's hand, he loses the fear of the darkness. God counters the spirit of fear with the privilege of sonship—of being one with his Son Jesus Christ. That relationship is simply but elegantly expressed in the children's song:

> Jesus loves me! this I know,
> For the Bible tells me so,
> Little ones to Him belong;
> They are weak but He is strong.

This song was written at West Point in the mid-nineteenth century by Miss Anna Warner, who lived on Constitution Island with her sister, Susan, for nearly seventy years. The Warner sisters taught Bible classes for cadets for many years, both at the Academy and at their island home. We enjoy today some of the fruits of their spiritual legacy. Through their influence many young officers went into the Army from West Point without fear, because of their faith in Jesus and in the Father's care.

3. *The system produces futility.*

> We know that the whole creation has been groaning as in the pains of childbirth right up to the present time. Not only so, but we ourselves, who have the firstfruits of the Spirit, groan inwardly as we wait eagerly for our adoption as sons, the redemption of our bodies. For in this hope we were saved . . . [Rom. 8:22–24, NIV].

Futility has become a way of life with many people who cannot cope with the system. They fight it, curse it, become angry and bitter. They are people without hope.

Earnest Levine, in his book *When Dreams and Heroes Died*, traced a generation of college students who lost hope because of their inability to alter the system. The result of their hopelessness was a passion to look out for themselves—for number one. Their objective in life was to go to college and get good grades, regardless of how they got them, so they could secure a good job, make lots of money, and buy a nice house. For this generation of collegians the future was "like riding first class on the Titanic."

When one has no hope, he or she is likely to embrace the philosophy that says, "Let us eat, drink, and be merry, for tomorrow we die." But into this world of futility, God has introduced the dynamic of hope. The same God who put the universe in place cares about you and me.

The same God "who raised Christ Jesus from the dead will give life to [our] mortal bodies also through his Spirit, which lives in [us]" (Rom. 8:11). Hope is alive today because God continues to work in the universe that he has made. Bill Gaither says it well in the contemporary chorus:

> Because He lives I can face tomorrow,
> Because He lives all fear is gone;
> Because I know He holds the future
> And life is worth the living—just because He lives.

4. *The system produces oppression of all kinds.* We see the symptoms of emptiness and hopelessness all around us. As he concludes this chapter of Romans, Paul writes: "Can anything separate us from the love of Christ? Can trouble, pain or persecution? Can lack of clothes and food, danger to life and limb, the threat of force of arms?" And his resounding answer to these questions is: "No, in all of these things we win an overwhelming victory through him who has proved his love for us." Nothing "in God's whole world has any power to separate us from the love of God in Jesus Christ our Lord!" (Rom. 8:35, 37, 39, *Phillips*). The Declaration of Independence is a proclamation of universal human rights and has given inspiration to oppressed peoples of every nation on this earth. But the liberating power of the love of Christ has gone beyond the heritage of free people to give meaning and hope to all people everywhere. Elsewhere Paul writes, "In this life we have three great lasting qualities—faith, hope and love. But the greatest of them is love" (1 Cor. 13:13, *Phillips*).

The good news for people everywhere is that God has put into effect a power that breaks the chains of the system. It liberates the human spirit and enables us to do all that we ought to do and all that God intends us to do.

In 1915, Constitution Island officially became a part of the West Point Military Reservation. The island, attached to West Point in the days of the American Revolution by a great chain, is now linked to West Point by a spiritual heritage that goes back to Anna and Susan Warner, who lived on the island for most of the nineteenth century. Their Christian influence and teaching centered on the gospel of Jesus Christ, which gives freedom from the chains of rebellion and fear and futility and oppression. We continue to practice that freedom, driven by the mandate of our Savior, the Light of the World, who said, "Let your light shine before men, that they may see your good deeds and praise your Father in heaven" (Matt. 5:16, NIV).

It is just a simple Sunday-school song, written by Susan Warner who, like her sister, was a prolific author as well as a gentle teacher. But the words serve as an ongoing challenge to pay the price of freedom.

> Jesus bids us shine with a clear, pure light,
> Like a little candle shining in the night.
> In this world of darkness we must shine!
> You, in your small corner, and I in mine.

19

Created for Good Works
R. Kent Hughes

We are his workmanship, created in Christ Jesus for good works, which God prepared beforehand, that we should walk in them.

Ephesians 2:10

Studs Terkel in his widely acclaimed oral history, *Working: People Talk About What They Do All Day and How They Feel About What They Do*, opens with these words: "This book, being about work, is by its very nature, about violence—to the spirit as well as to the body. It is about ulcers as well as accidents. About shouting matches as well as fist fights. About nervous breakdowns as well as kicking the dog around. It is, above all (or beneath all), about daily humiliations."

Today, millions of people regard their work as something they must bear, a living indignity. Their feelings are not without precedent. The novelist Herman Melville felt much the same: "They talk of dignity of work, bosh. The dignity is in the leisure." And Thoreau said, "The laboring man has not leisure for a true integrity day by day. He has not time to be anything but a machine."

Strong statements. But there is equal eloquence among those holding the opposite opinion. Historian Thomas Carlyle wrote: "There is a perennial nobleness, and even sacredness in work . . . In idleness alone is their perpetual despair. . . . A man perfects himself by working. All work, even cotton spinning, is noble. Work alone is noble."

In our own time, David Ben Gurion, pioneer leader of Israel, said: "We don't consider manual work as a curse, or a bitter necessity, not

149

even as a means of making a living. We consider it as a high human function. As a basis of human life. The most dignified thing in the life of a human being and which ought to be free, creative. Man ought to be proud of it."

There are, indeed, impassioned competing perspectives about work. The importance of how we regard it is obvious, for of our sixteen daily waking hours, many of us spend eight to twelve of them at work, five or six days a week. And many who are not formally employed work just as much. We cannot escape the fact that how we regard our work conditions most of our waking hours.

So the question we want to consider is this: How ought we to regard work? Specifically, how ought we to regard the work we are paid to do, and the work we are not paid to do, such as that which we do in our homes and community and church?

The text that best answers these questions is Paul's great declaration on work in Ephesians 2:10: "We are his workmanship, created in Christ Jesus for good works, which God prepared beforehand, that we should walk in them."

First we will consider what this declaration means, for it contains some sublimely elevating truths. Then we will consider our responsibility as Christians in the presence of such a great declaration.

A Sublime Declaration About Work

We are introduced to the meaning of this remarkable text by the mounting force of the context in this second chapter of Ephesians. The chapter begins by describing the *amazing depths* to which the Ephesians had fallen. They were dead in their sins, under the sway of Satan, and bound by their lusts. They were children of wrath. Then, surprisingly, Paul elevates them from these amazing depths to *amazing heights* as he seats them in the heavenly places next to Christ, in whom they have become alive (Eph. 2:1–6). "By grace you have been saved through faith; and this is not your own doing, it is the gift of God—not because of works, lest any man should boast" (Eph. 2:8–9). It is all of God. Nothing comes from man. Finally, in our text we have this *amazing declaration*: "We are his workmanship, created in Christ Jesus for good works, which God prepared beforehand, that we should walk in them."

The sublime truth of this driving context is that man is so hopelessly lost that he can do nothing to merit salvation. But God, by his grace, does what man cannot do—even exalting man to "heavenly places."

Although we must never think that we can earn salvation by our own good works, we should also realize that after salvation good works must follow, for the context culminates in the declaration that "we are his workmanship, created . . . for good works." Grace makes us want to do good works.

This truth is a remarkable revelation of the state of our hearts, because one of the sure marks of a healthy spiritual life is that we want to do good works for God—not for what we can get, but because we love him. The words of our text show us how deeply implanted in the heart of a believer this inclination to do good works is.

The word *workmanship* is especially revealing. The Greek from which this word comes is "*poiema*," from which we derive our English word *poem*. It means "that which has been made—a work," while sometimes it even means "a poem." The old Scottish name for a poet was "a maker." In fact, in one of his novels, Sir Walter Scott had one of his characters say to another, who had just given a beautiful description of a city, "Aha, so thou can'st play the maker yet?" Then Scott adds a footnote explaining that the ancient Scottish word for "poet" is "maker," which is the literal translation of the Greek *poietes*.

Because of this, some have tried to replace "workmanship" (as our translation renders it) with "poem," so that it reads "we are his poem." The result is misleading, however because *poiema* in Greek meant much more than written lines. It meant any and every work of art. It could mean a statue or a song or architecture. The best translation by far is that given by F. F. Bruce: "his work of art, his masterpiece." *We are God's work of art*.

I do not think that there is any more exalted description of the believer in all of Scripture. You are God's work of art! I am God's work of art! The implications of this ought to make our believing hearts sing. We are presently being fashioned by God into masterpieces that will be completed in eternity. Each of us shall be a work of beauty. We shall all bear a divinely wrought uniqueness. As an artist, God takes great pride in us. We increasingly bear the marks of his hands.

That we are his work of art calls up the Old Testament metaphor of God as the Potter and ourselves as the clay. Whereas a potter does his work *externally*, the divine Potter molds us from *within*. Whereas a human potter works *on* the clay, our Potter works *in* the clay of our lives. He kneads his Spirit into us as we lie on his workbench, and the Spirit passes through and into us and gives our clay its form as it is shaped on his wheel.

It is through the work of God's Son that it becomes possible for us to be made works of art. "We are his workmanship," says the apostle, and then follows with the phrase "created in Christ Jesus." We can be made works of art because we are "in" Christ. In 2 Corinthians 5:17, Paul says, "Therefore, if any one is in Christ, he is a new creation; the old has passed away, behold, the new has come." Because we are God's works of art, the Eternal Artist is putting his beauty in us. He is expressing his thought through us. He is making his music out of us. We are his work of art.

A Sublime Responsibility to Work

What, then, is our responsibility as Christians in light of this great declaration?

The result of this dizzying reality is that we naturally do good works. As God's masterpieces, we are "created in Christ Jesus *for good works,* which God prepared beforehand, that we should walk in them." We show off his artistry by the works we perform. His work *in* us produces his work *through* us. It is that simple.

This does not mean that every good work done by us is contained in a thought of God, as if written in a book. But it does mean that we are perfectly equipped for whatever may come our way—to do good works. There is not a situation in which we do not have the power to do good works. In fact, we *must* do them. Our good works amount to God's signature of authenticity on our lives. Others know that we are real "signed" works of God by what we do. This is what the apostle's great declaration means in our lives.

First, we have a sacred duty to be good workers in the marketplace—the place where we receive wages. Neither the present text, nor any other, allows for the division of life into separate sacred and secular spheres. It is foreordained that we are to walk in good works. The Christian does good works wherever he goes. As an employee, his good works permeate his work so that his work is good. Martin Luther gave this truth classic expression when he said:

> Your work is a very sacred matter. God delights in it, and through it He wants to bestow His blessing on you. This praise of work should be inscribed on all tools, on the forehead and the faces that sweat from toiling. For the world does not consider labor blessing.

Luther's words are true. This does not mean, however, that work is to become an end in itself. True as the Reformation and Puritan work ethic may be in its original purity, industry readily perverted it to the worship of work. In fact, it can easily be demonstrated that in the eighteenth and nineteenth centuries this work ethic came to provide a theological guise for addiction to power and wealth—and the exploitation of workers.

Anytime work is seen as an end in itself, it leads to exploitation. Karl Marx carried this ideology of work to its ultimate extreme. According to him, man is what he does at his work. Work is the exceptional virtue. It is "the secularization of the idea of the divine vocation of man in work." When we see work as everything, we are no better than the Marxists and, because of our calling, we are worse.

Nor should the sacredness of work lead us to romanticizing about work. A well-traveled parable tells of three workmen building a cathedral who were questioned by a visitor as to what they were doing. The first answered, "I am chipping these stones." The second answered, "I am earning wages." The third man answered, "I am building a great cathedral." The traditional application holds up the third man as the great example of the proper attitude toward work.

The story is good, as far as it goes. But all workmen are *not* building cathedrals. Some here in Chicago work in the sewers amidst the city's waste. Others dig holes and then fill them up. We must realize that the second workman's perspective is also noble. There are men and women who are glorifying God in their "nothing" jobs simply because they are earning wages to take home to their families.

The truth is, we glorify God when we realize that our work is not an end in itself, when we refuse to romanticize about its nobility—all jobs are not noble—and then do our best to the glory of God. Christians ought to be the best workers wherever they are: the best in attitude, the best in dependability, the best in their integrity. They ought to have even the best sweat. Paul says, "Whatever your task, work heartily, as serving the Lord and not men, knowing that from the Lord you will receive the inheritance as your reward; you are serving the Lord Christ" (Col. 3:23–24; cf. Eph. 6:5–9).

Gerard Manley Hopkins put it this way:

> Smiting on an anvil, sawing a beam, white-washing a wall, driving horses, sweeping, scouring, everything gives God some glory if being in

His grace you do it as your duty. To go to Communion worthily gives God great glory, but to take food in thankfulness and temperance gives Him glory too. To lift up the hands in prayer gives God glory, but a man with a dungfork in his hand, a woman with a slop pail, give Him glory too. He is so great that all things give Him glory if you mean they should. So then, my brethren, live.

As God's works of art, created in Christ for good works, let us show the way to a tired, bitter world. This is the way all of us should approach our regular duties at home and in our neighborhood. God must be glorified in all things.

If Paul's great declaration calls us to account in our daily work in the world, even more does it do so in our church work—activities that are obviously spiritual. Here we must understand that no one is exempted because of commitments outside the church. Other commitments do not rule out service in the church.

While all of life is to be lived to the glory of God, not all jobs are as important spiritually as others. The church, by its nature, is a repository of the important things of life. What we do or do not do for our church has profound spiritual consequences.

Too many people today are spiritual hitchhikers. They come along for the ride, but never offer to wash the windshield—and certainly never pay for the gas. The great English preacher Charles Spurgeon called them "feeders" and chastized them in quaint but forceful language:

> I know that in many churches the main thing is to sit in a corner pew, and be fed. Well, of course, every creature needs to be fed, from the pig upwards—you must excuse my mentioning that unclean animal, for he is the creature whose principal business it is to feed, and he is not a nice creature at all, and I do not at all admire Christian people whose one business is to feed and feed. Why, I have heard them even grumble at a sermon that was meant for the conversion of sinners, because they thought there was no food for them in it! They are great receptacles of food; but Dear Christian people, do not any of you live merely to feed—not even on heavenly food; but if God be with you, as you say he is, then get to His work.

How we are challenged by the intense labors of those who have gone before us to build the church! Our Lord set a beautiful example in his willingness to dialogue with the woman at the well. John says that

Jesus "sat thus on the well" (John 4:6, KJV), which indicates that Jesus had plopped down like a weary man does at the end of a hard day's work. When the Samaritan woman approached, he could easily have ignored her. But he did not. Despite his exhaustion, he began on one of the most intense cases of spiritual aggression in all Scripture. Jesus gave his all, even when tired. He said, "The Son of man came not to be served but to serve . . ." (Matt. 20:28) and, "We must work the works of him who sent me, while it is day; night comes, when no one can work" (John 9:4).

Paul, too, lived like his Savior: "You remember our labor and toil, brethren; we worked night and day, that we might not burden any of you, while we preached to you the gospel of God" (1 Thess. 2:9; cf. 2 Thess. 3:8).

All the great ones of the church have followed in the footsteps of Christ and his apostles. Calvin labored twelve to eighteen hours a day as a preacher, professor of theology, superintendent of churches, municipal advisor, and regulator of public morals. His correspondence was second only to that of the scholar Erasmus.

John Wesley preached 42,000 sermons and rode horseback an average of 4,500 miles a year. Often he rode sixty to seventy miles a day and almost always preached three times each day.

That great expositor of Scripture, Alexander Maclaren, always wore workman's boots in his study to remind him what he was there for. He once spent sixty hours in preparation of a single sermon.

Charles Spurgeon was once so tired he preached a sermon in his sleep. His wife wrote down the main points, and he went to church and preached it!

Created for Good Works

Do not succumb to thinking that the work of the church is to be left to the professionals. Every believer owes a substantial part of his or her time and energy to working for the cause of Christ. Have you ever thought what would happen if every church attender gave one hour a week to the Lord? In our church alone that would total 1,400 hours a week, 5,600 hours a month, and 72,800 hours a year. At minimum wage that comes to $244,000 a year.

Some of you need to get involved. God wants to use your gifts to build his church. Some are already doing too much. If you are one of these, don't listen. But others need to heed the voice of God.

Brothers and sisters, listen to this: "We are his workmanship"—his work of art—"created in Christ Jesus for good works, which God prepared beforehand, that we should walk in them." What a declaration! We are the ones who are to sing his song in the world. We are to help others see the rhythm of the Divine.

As the Master Artisan, God delights in us. He takes great pride in us. He is constantly adding his finishing touches.

Because we are his work, let us walk in the good works, which he has prepared beforehand. The power comes from him.

We can do it in the marketplace, in our homes, and in our church.

20

A Taste of the Future
Theodore M. *Olsen*

And when the hour came, he sat at table, and the apostles with him. And he said to them, "I have earnestly desired to eat this passover with you before I suffer; for I tell you I shall not eat it until it is fulfilled in the kingdom of God."
Luke 22:14–16

The Seder of the Passover is now complete,
According to the laws, rules and customs.
As we have been privileged to celebrate it this year,
May we be worthy to actually offer it in the Holy Land.
O Pure One, who abides in the Temple,
Raise up Thy numberless people,
O speedily lead the branches Thou hast planted,
As free men to Zion, with songs of rejoicing.
NEXT YEAR IN JERUSALEM![1]

With these words, the Passover meal is finished, not with a reminder of the past but with the longing for what is yet to be. In this spirit of happy expectation, Jewish families rise from the table and continue their festivities well into the night, singing lively songs of joy. "Next year in Jerusalem!"

Our text reminds us that the Communion Service was conceived in the womb of the Passover. Like the Passover, the Lord's Supper both commemorates and anticipates. In its eating and drinking, those who

1. Ruth Gruber Fredman, *The Passover Seder* (Philadelphia: University of Pennsylvania, 1981), p. 87.

offer thanks for past deliverance sharpen their vision of the future. They leave the table filled with the hope of future deliverance. God is not finished yet!

That morsel of bread, that sip of wine—these are the Christian's taste of the future. "Next time in heaven!" Thus the apostle Paul wrote, "Whenever you eat this bread and drink this cup, you proclaim the Lord's death until he comes" (1 Cor. 11:26, NIV). The Communion Service is the appetizer. We wait with joyous expectation for the banquet.

Like the Passover, the Lord's Supper is the meal of exiles. It nourishes the hope of believers, for whom the coming kingdom of God is always on the horizon. The Communion Service keeps us in touch with our homeland.

It is not a feast of fantasy. At his last Passover our Lord rooted this prophecy firmly in history. "This is my body given for you . . ." (Luke 22:19, NIV). Our hope rests secure upon the facts of the death and resurrection of Jesus Christ. "We believe that Jesus died and rose again and so we believe that God will bring with Jesus those who have fallen asleep in him" (1 Thess. 4:14, NIV).

For this reason, each Communion Service ends with the implied affirmation: "Next time in heaven!" The Bible closes with the prayer "Amen. Come, Lord Jesus" (Rev. 22:20). Capturing this flavor, the Communion liturgy of the Moravian Brethren concludes with this pronouncement: "Till He come to the great supper at which, in the banqueting hall of the consummation, His Bride will behold Him closely. Come, Lord Jesus! The Bride calls!"

In two thousand years, the need for the Communion Service's perennial focus on the future was never more urgent than today. Our self-absorbed, two-dimensional culture is not inclined to look beyond the flat little world of human creation. As Christians, our thoughts of heaven are often vague and fleeting.

Philip Yancey has commented on the lack of literary interest in heaven. In recent years, he tells us, no articles on the future life are recorded in the *Reader's Guide to Periodical Literature* and only a handful in the *Religion Index to Periodicals*.[2] Yancey goes on to suggest reasons for the contemporary disinterest in heaven. One is affluence. What can heaven possibly offer that might interest us? What more do we need? Another reason is paganism. By this he means that our passive surrender to death as the natural completion of life has preempted our con-

---

2. Philip Yancey, "Heaven Can't Wait," *Christianity Today,* September 7, 1984: 53.

cern with heaven. Certainly we can learn much from the research of Elisabeth Kubler-Ross and others about the stages of dying, but acceptance of death is not life's final goal.

Listen to C. S. Lewis's exhortation as he opens his chapter on "Hope."

> Hope is one of the Theological virtues. This means that a continual looking forward to the eternal world is not (as some modern people think) a form of escapism or wishful thinking, but one of the things a Christian is meant to do. It does not mean that we are to leave the present world as it is. If you read history you will find that the Christians who did most for the present world were just those who thought most of the next. The Apostles themselves who set on foot the conversion of the Roman Empire, the great men who built up the Middle Ages, the English Evangelicals who abolished the Slave Trade, all left their mark on Earth, precisely because their minds were occupied with Heaven. It is since Christians have largely ceased to think of the other world that they have been so ineffective in this. Aim at Heaven, and you will get earth 'thrown in': aim at earth and you will get neither.[3]

How easily earth spoils our appetite for heaven. Our desire for the future needs the stimulant of the bread and the cup.

A Taste of Perfect Fellowship

"When the hour came, Jesus and his apostles reclined at the table. And he said to them, 'I have eagerly desired to eat this Passover with you before I suffer'" (NIV). That thirteen Jewish men should gather at sunset for the Passover was unprecendented. Passover is a family affair. All across the biblical world the children of Israel gathered as households, as they still do today, on this night to be observed to the Lord for bringing them out from the land of Egypt (Exod. 12:42).

But Jesus broke the tradition. He revealed his heart when he said to his disciples, "With desire I have desired to eat this passover with you . . ." (Luke 22:15, KJV). That is, "You are my family."

Eating a common meal is the universal symbol of the bonds of love and friendship. The dining table is the place of acceptance, comfort, and security. Do you remember the emblem of the Walton family's to-

---

3. C. S. Lewis, *Mere Christianity* (London: Fontana, 1952), p. 116.

getherness in the television series? That massive kitchen table: see the clan seated happily together at dinner! Like the Passover, the Lord's Supper celebrates social as well as spiritual nurture. It symbolizes communion both with Christ and with his brothers and sisters.

Communion is served at the only table long enough to encircle the globe. Today we take our places in anticipation of Jesus' great expectation: "I say to you that many will come from the east and the west, and will take their places at the feast with Abraham, Isaac and Jacob in the kingdom of heaven" (Matt. 8:11, NIV).

The time will come when all other families, tribes, and nations will have served their temporal purposes and only Christ's church will remain. How our Lord longs for that final gathering of his family! Communion is a taste of perfect fellowship.

But look at the dissension around the first Communion Table: "Also a dispute arose among them as to which of them was considered to be greatest" (Luke 22:24, NIV). Imagine that! A family feud at the Last Supper!

The Lord's Table at the church in Corinth was also split by discord. Christians were treating one another like strangers, if not enemies. What they called "the Lord's Supper" was a farce (1 Cor. 11:20–21).

The Apostles' Creed expresses our fundamental convictions. "I believe . . . in the communion of saints," it says. If, indeed, we do believe in the communion of saints, then this taste of future fellowship whets our appetite not only for heaven, but for the enrichment of our relationship with fellow Christians today. The bread and cup are emblems of what is yet to be and at the same time persuade us of what ought to be in our relationships today.

We have no misgivings, no delusions of perfection this side of heaven. We will not take ourselves too seriously. After all,

> To live with the saints in heaven will be glory,
> But to live with the saints on earth
> Is often another story.

Nevertheless, the image of what is yet to be does profoundly impress itself upon what is. We are saved by hope from our self-centered pettiness. Paul wrote to the Colossians that "the love you have for all the saints . . . spring[s] from the hope that is stored up for you in heaven . . ." (Col. 1:4–5, NIV).

> Blest be the tie that binds
> Our hearts in Christian love;
> The fellowship of kindred minds
> Is like to that above.

Whenever we are at home together around the Communion Table, we are reminded, "Next time in heaven!" Communion is a taste of perfect fellowship.

A Taste of Perfect Fulfillment

". . . I shall not eat [the Passover] until it is fulfilled in the kingdom of God." This is Jesus' solemn vow of reunion after the agony and separation of his passion. The final deliverance of the people of God as foretold in the symbols of the Passover and Communion services will be realized. We have his word!

At his second coming, the tokens of bread and wine will give way to the real presence of the living Christ. The prophecy of communion will be fulfilled. For the Christian, that is heaven: the presence of Christ, the Beatific Vision: ". . . we shall see him as he is" (1 John 3:2, NIV).

The Bible delights in the picture of a banquet, hosted by God himself, to describe the joy of heaven. "Blessed are those who are invited to the wedding supper of the Lamb!" (Rev. 19:9, NIV). The Lord's Supper is a foretaste of the Lamb's Supper. We come to the table with a heightened awareness of the presence of God. We relish the tiny bite of bread and shallow sip of wine as a feast of rich satisfaction. Indeed, we associate the very aroma of the cup itself with absolute contentment in Christ.

Why is this simple memorial service so fulfilling? Because it excites our appetites for what is yet to come.

The Christian at the Communion Service is a study in contradictions. He professes complete satisfaction in Christ, yet, at the same time, hungers and thirsts for more of Christ. In fact, the lack of such desire is a sign of ill health. Spiritual complacency is the deadliest of sins. A thousand years ago, Bernard of Clairvaux captured the essence of normal Christian experience in these lines:

> We taste Thee, O thou living Bread,
> And long to feast upon Thee still;
> We drink of Thee, the Fountainhead,
> And thirst our souls from Thee to fill.

Perhaps you have seen the picture portraying an artist's interpretation of the lavish feast of heaven, when the longing after Christ will be completely satisfied. It is a magnificent banquet—suspended in ethereal space—set with the finest china, crystal, linen, golden candelabra, and silverware. Striking carved chairs, awaiting the guests' arrival, surround the table. The vivid scene is painted against the backdrop of a glorious sunlit sky. Underneath, the caption reads: "All Is Now Ready."

Through the centuries, the hope of Passover's final fulfillment impelled the nation of Israel forward in its mission. Christ has designed the Communion to remind us of our destiny as the children of God. His purpose is to motivate us to realize that destiny in communion with himself and with his family even now.

A father promised his eight-year-old son a weekend vacation. They would go to a very special place together. The night before they left, the boy came to his father and sat excitedly in his lap. He looked up and said with sparkling eyes, "Dad, thank you for tomorrow."

How excited are you about tomorrow? How captivated by the Father's plans? How hungry and thirsty for heaven's banquet?

If you read history, you will find that the Christians who did most for the present world were just those who thought most of the next.

The Word and the sacrament unite to declare that eternal life has already begun. Christ's people are meant to experience its fullness now: to live with "one foot in heaven," in fellowship with him and with all who belong to him.

Communion is just the taste of the future we need. Whenever we eat this bread and drink this cup, we do so with the knowledge that there's more to come—much, much more. *Next time in heaven!*

21

Losing Your Life for Christ's Sake
Charles W. Colson

"For whoever wishes to save his life shall lose it; but whoever loses his life for My sake shall find it."

Matthew 16:25 (NASB)

Whoever loses his life for My sake shall find it." How Christ turns the world on its head! How much there is to understand here, how deep and rich this teaching of our Lord!

I am not a theologian, so the message I bring today does not purport to be a scholarly exegesis. I can, however, witness to the power of this truth in my own life. In fact, if my life stands for anything at all, it is literal truth of what Jesus told his disciples. Let me explain.

A few years ago we celebrated the tenth anniversary of the Watergate break-in. Because of my association with that infamous event, the press chased me around everywhere, trying to discover some newsworthy reflections from the White House "hatchet man." One reporter asked, "What was the message of Watergate for you?"

I answered, much to his amazement, that the message for me was that of Alexander Solzhenitsyn, who wrote after his deliverance from a Soviet prison camp, "Bless you, prison, bless you for having been in my life!"

I can look back and say, "Bless you, Watergate, for having been in my life." Why? Because Watergate led to prison, and it was in prison that I learned, as Solzhenitsyn wrote, that the "object of life is not prosperity, as we are made to believe, but the maturing of the soul." It was in my prison experience that I saw that the meaning of life is not found in pursuit of gain, but in the service of Jesus Christ.

This came home to me in a very personal way on Easter several years ago. Every Easter I go into a prison. Where better to celebrate the victory of an empty tomb than in one of the tombs of our own society? I arrived at 6:00 A.M. at Michigan City Prison, was escorted through all of the security checkpoints, and finally reached the prison auditorium. There I saw more than three hundred inmates. What a joyous experience! Those men had to be up at 5:00 A.M. to attend, and people normally sleep late in prison. It really meant something for those inmates to be there.

As I walked in, one tough-looking convict came running over toward me. "Hey, Mr. Colson," he shouted, "remember when you were here a year ago?"

"Sure do," I replied. We had offered a Prison Fellowship in-prison seminar. At the closing I had told the men about the two thieves crucified with Jesus. The first thief refused to understand who Christ was; the second repented and said, "Jesus, remember me when You come in Your kingdom!" (Luke 23:42, NASB). I had said to the inmates, "Go back to your cells tonight and be like that second thief. Christ will come into your life, just as he did for that thief on the cross."

"I did it; I went back to my cell and prayed," the prisoner before me continued excitedly. "And ever since, they've had my body in this place—but not me!"

What a witness to the power of Jesus Christ! As I looked at this joyous brother—and the hundreds of others like him—I could not help thinking about my own life.

It seemed the classic story: the poor kid who grows up in the Depression, works his way through an Ivy League college, becomes the youngest administrative assistant in the U.S. Senate, earns a doctorate of law at night. It was the American dream fulfilled: the climb to the top, member of the board of directors of major corporations while still in my thirties, head of a large law firm. I argued cases before the highest courts in the land and won them. Finally, at age thirty-nine, I came to the White House to work for the president of the United States, playing a key role in the most powerful office in the world.

But, as I reflected on my life, I realized that my real legacy is none of my successes or achievements, but that I was a convict who went to prison. God has chosen my one great defeat as the thing that he has used to touch the lives of thousands.

I remember hanging on my prison bars and saying, "God, get us out of here; you know we are wasting our time in this prison!" How God must laugh at man's wisdom. And so often he will use that which we least expect so the glory will go to him, not us. It's the supreme illustration of the paradox of which Jesus speaks here in Matthew 16.

Thus, what matters in life is not what we do, but what a sovereign God may choose to do through us. What *really* counts is our obedience and our right relationship with the living God, that we are faithful to what he commands. We must lose our life in order to find it, because he will use our brokenness, that which often we least expect, for his purposes. It is difficult, almost impossible, in this success-oriented, materialistic culture for us to understand what that truth is all about.

We mistakenly suppose that our successes, our plans, are going to change the world. We live in the era that the great French historian Jacques Ellul calls "the political illusion." We are persuaded that there is a political solution to every problem, when, in fact, there most certainly is not. The roots of our problems today are spiritual and moral.

When I was in the White House, I saw how impotent government can be. Every morning, precisely at 8:00, the ten senior advisors to the president of the United States would gather around a huge, gleaming mahogany table in the Roosevelt Room. And every morning the same scenario would take place. Henry Kissinger would hurry in, out of breath, briefing books under each arm, and take his place at the long table. He would turn to the president and announce, "Mr. President, the decisions we make today will shape the course of history." Five days a week, fifty-two weeks a year!

But when I left the White House, one reason I felt so empty inside was the knowledge of how little we really did change. Sure, we sponsored some laws and introduced some policies, but for the most part, what we dealt with revolved around acquiring and maintaining our own power.

When I was in prison, however, I saw something different. In prison men and women live with an awful sense of isolation and hopelessness, the stale odors from the open urinals, the guards coming around shining flashlights in the inmates' eyes, the dreadful despair. Because of that, people give up and simply lie on their bunks twenty out of twenty-four hours a day, their bodies and souls corroding. I would watch those men, their families breaking up at home, with nothing to live for in prison, and I would ask myself, "What hope is there?"

I met one man my first night in prison. He and I became brothers in Christ. Soon a small group of us began meeting: three blacks, four whites, two convicted dope pushers, a car thief, a stock swindler, and a former special counsel to the president of the United States.

Night after night, as we were praying, men would come in and ask us what we were doing. We would tell them all about repentance, not just for the crime that got them into the prison, but repentance for the sin that marks all our lives: repentance before a holy God. Then we would tell them how the living God could transform their lives.

I would see those men who had been living corpses, lying on their bunks, walking through that institution with their heads down. Then, the next day, they would be up and around that prison with their heads up, transformed by the power of the living God. There in prison, the ultimate illustration of where government institutions cannot deal with moral problems nor change the human heart, I saw that God's way worked, that God will transform people by the power of the living Christ. This is our hope today: the power of the gospel to transform lives and change the values by which we live in this society.

Alexander Solzhenitsyn, perhaps the greatest prophetic voice in the world today, has a simple saying. During his childhood in Russia, when there were natural disasters, accidents, or problems, the people had an explanation: "Men have forgotten God."

"If I were to survey all of the 20th century," Solzhenitzyn says, "I would have to say that the Russian proverb sums it up: 'Men have forgotten God.'" He is right.

My brothers and sisters, we are engaged in spiritual warfare. We have the weapons and the opportunity, as the church of Jesus Christ, to present a moral and spiritual message to a sick and needy nation. The answers will not come from the institutions and the temples of power. They can only come from our churches: the message that one must lose his life in order to find it. That is our only hope.

But this hope will not be realized unless the church becomes what God has called us to be. Tragically, in our time we have become conformed to the world, molded as one of society's institutions, another organization, another bureaucracy.

But the church of Jesus Christ is not just another organization; it is an organism. It is the dwelling place of the living God and the living witness of a whole new kingdom. The apostle Peter said to the church,

"You are a chosen race, a royal priesthood, a holy nation" (1 Peter 2:9). I love that phrase—"holy nation." God used it with Moses at Sinai when he called out his chosen people. In the holy nation covenant God originally made, he first called out his people and then promised that he would build his tabernacle and pitch his tent. He would "dwell among" his people (Exod. 29:45). The promise of the sovereign God is that he would come and actually take up residence, pitch his tent among his chosen people. That is a staggering thought.

In the New Testament, God makes the same covenant. "And the Word became flesh and dwelt among us . . ." John says (John 1:14). The Greek word for "dwelt" translates literally "to pitch a tent." So the "holy nation" is the same covenant people. Only now, not just the Jew but the Gentile also, free man and slave, from east and west.

So, too, in Revelation 21:3, when John gives us the description of the new heaven, he writes, "Behold, the tabernacle of God is among men, and He shall dwell among them . . ." (NASB). *He shall dwell among his people.* The word *dwell* here again means literally that God will pitch his tent among his people.

Peter understood this when he spoke of the new covenant. How ironic that it would be Peter who would remind the church of its role as the holy nation. For, of all the apostles, Peter was the most Jewish. He was the one God had to hit over the head three times to get him to preach the good news to the Gentiles in Caesarea (Acts 10:1–23). Peter was the one who had the circumcision dispute with Paul (Gal. 2:11–14). He, of all the apostles, would be the one least expected to step forward and say to churches all over the then-known world, "You are a holy nation."

From these passages we are taught that what distinguishes Christianity is not that it is simply another religion, not just another book of benign proverbs, not simply a creed by which people live. What distinguishes Christianity is that the Creator of this universe has chosen to dwell in our midst and to call us out to be his holy nation, a separate people, a kingdom of his own choosing.

This absolutely transcendent thought means that we must pay first loyalty to the kingdom of God above all else. There is no greater challenge to the church of Jesus Christ today than to be what God intends it to be—his visible presence on earth as the holy nation of his own chosen people.

How are we to do this? It will be only by God's grace. Yet the calling to lose our lives for Christ's sake, and thereby be transformed into a holy nation, requires that we must work to display God's grace to the world. Today, I want to suggest five ways this can be done in these last years of the twentieth century.

First, we must discern the false values of our culture and clearly reject them. The saddest thing in the world today is to see the egocentricity and materialism that have so pervaded America. Our best-seller books are all "What's in it for you?" literature: *Winning Through Intimidation; Looking Out for Number One.* Pay fifteen dollars for *The One-Minute Manager* and you can learn how to succeed at anything and quickly. Our culture bombards us with the message that we are self-sufficient to rise to the top. Of course, the gospel of Jesus Christ is the exact antithesis of this. It says we must lose ourselves. We must bear one another's burdens. We Christians must proclaim this truth and teach our people to discern and reject the false values of this culture. We must live only by God's values, not the world's.

The second thing we must do is take our stand upon the holy, inerrant Word of God. We don't have anything else. When I became a Christian, there was no issue that I struggled with harder than what to do with the Bible. That answer, I found, is clear from the historical evidence: It is God's very Word. I read and re-read this Holy Book. It changes and challenges my life every day. Thus I defend this Book and live under its authority.

Of course, I do this because of the example of our Master. Jesus said to the Father, "Thy word is truth" (John 17:17). Jesus treated the Bible as *the* authority, as the infallible revelation of God. I can do no less. Following Christ means we follow his pattern of living according to the revelation given by the Father.

Third, we must take this Word, and the church that is built upon it, to the people. Again, Jesus Christ is our example. Jesus went into the home of the most notorious sinners in town. He went where the sick, the lame, and the hurting were. He went among the outcasts and the lepers. He didn't set up an office and say, "Come into the temple, so that I can tell you the good news." He went out and lived with the people, identified with them, and was in fellowship with their suffering.

If we are to follow Christ, we must go out to the unevangelized millions of this world who are hurting and suffering. They may never come into our gilded sanctuaries, but if we take the gospel to them, we will see a spiritual explosion, as the church comes alive in faithfulness to Christ.

Fourth, we must be holy. The essence of the covenant in which the living

God tells us he will live in our midst is that we are to "be holy," for he is holy (Lev. 11:44). My friends, we must be witnesses to the holiness of God. And not only in our personal piety, our codes of do's and don'ts, for when God talks about holiness, he means something much more. He means doing justice among people. Holiness is living by God's standards of righteousness.

Consider Solomon's prayer that he might be given wisdom to administer justice among God's people. Because of his desire for justice, which was obviously pleasing to God, God favored him (1 Kings 3:3–14). The command of God is that we not sell the poor for a pair of shoes; that we model our courts as true halls of justice; that we serve the needy; that we care for the widows and orphans; that we cease doing evil and do good—that in everything righteousness may abound in the land, not just in individual witness, but in our lives together as the people of God.

Finally, we are called to be not just hearers, but doers of the Word. Perhaps an illustration from the work of Prison Fellowship will help. We brought six convicts out of a prison in Atlanta. We called up six Atlanta volunteer families and asked if they would take these inmates into their homes. Not a single family asked the color of the convict's skin or the crime he had committed. The inmates—two black, two white, two Hispanic—moved into our volunteers' homes. Every morning at 9:00, they studied the Bible together. At 11:00 A.M. they put on their coveralls and went to work on the homes of two elderly widows in inner-city Atlanta. They put in insulation, weatherized, painted, and in two weeks did what those widows had been waiting eighteen months for some government agency to do. That is the church showing what it means to be a doer of the Word. It was a powerful witness, a great demonstration of an alternative to incarceration, but also something much more.

One of the widows was Roxie Vaughn, eighty-two years old, blind from birth. We told her, "Roxie, we are coming in to restore your house and winterize it." Roxie was delighted. "Six convicts will supply the labor," we continued; then she turned ashen white. You see, Roxie's home had been burglarized four times in the previous two years. But the third day those convicts were in her house there was Roxie playing her small electric organ, and there were the six prisoners behind her singing "Amazing Grace." That is the reconciling power of the gospel!

The church service we held when we sent those convicts back to prison after two weeks was one of the most joyous experiences of my life. The volunteers' kids were saying, "Don't let Johnny go back to prison." The widows were embracing the volunteers, and the volunteers were embracing the convicts. What we saw was the witness of the "holy nation" at work in that community, reconciling differences, doing the Word of God, being the salt and light, making a difference for Christ.

That is our call; that is our command. We are not to be simply another institution of society. We are to be a whole new and different order. As John Calvin said, we are to be the invisible kingdom of God made visible on this earth. This is our challenge. This is God's Word to his church today.

We must hurry to accept this challenge. Why? For four years I walked around beside a man who carried in his pocket a small code card. Behind us walked a man with a little black box. With a code from that card, the president of the United States could set off a signal inside that black box that within twenty minutes would unleash nuclear destruction against the Soviet Union. In the Kremlin they have exactly the same kind of rig. The president, like all presidents, worked hard to avoid this horrible possibility. Yet, if you look through the pages of history, you will see that never has man failed to visit his inhumanity on his fellowman. So sinful are we that we will go to all lengths to do evil. We now have the technology to keep up with our depravity, the capacity within a button's reach to obliterate utterly the human race.

If there is any hope, it is not in the institutions of power. It is not in strategic-arms talks. It is not in the good will of people, because we are not good. We are all, at heart, sinners. The only place there is hope is in the redeeming power of the gospel of Jesus Christ to save us from our own self-destruction. If we, of ourselves, try to save our lives, we will lose them. Only if we live our lives for Christ's sake and become a holy nation, only then will we bring life to a dying world. May God make us determined that, having heard his Word, we are going to be a holy nation, visible and plain to all on this earth.

22

It Is Written
David Ralph Barnhart

Then Jesus was led by the Spirit into the desert to be tempted by the devil. After fasting forty days and forty nights, he was hungry. The tempter came to him and said, "If you are the Son of God, tell these stones to become bread."

Jesus answered, "It is written: 'Man does not live on bread alone, but on every word that comes from the mouth of God.'"

Then the devil took him to the holy city and had him stand on the highest point of the temple. "If you are the Son of God," he said, "throw yourself down. For it is written: 'He will command his angels concerning you, and they will lift you up in their hands, so that you will not strike your foot against a stone.'"

Jesus answered him, "It is also written: 'Do not put the Lord your God to the test.'"

Again, the devil took him to a very high mountain and showed him all the kingdoms of the world and their splendor. "All this I will give you," he said, "if you will bow down and worship me."

Jesus said to him, "Away from me, Satan! For it is written: 'Worship the Lord your God, and serve him only.'"

Then the devil left him, and angels came and attended him.

Matthew 4:1–11 (NIV)

Nearly two thousand years ago, Satan engaged our Lord in deadly combat in the wilderness of Judea. Nearly five hundred years ago, Satan tried unsuccessfully to destroy the church as he faced that great defender of the faith, Martin Luther. In similar struggles over the centuries against scores of brave Christian warriors, Satan has launched waves of fierce attacks, winning a skirmish here and there, but always losing in the end. Defeat has seemingly not discouraged him. He continues still to fight the people of God at every turn.

One of the greatest battles ever waged against the church is being waged today. Amazingly, countless numbers of Christians seem totally unaware of the tumult, while others shrug their shoulders in an attitude of indifference. With little resistance in many quarters of the church, Satan, with his demonic legions and eager allies, has launched an all-out offensive to seize control of the church of Jesus Christ and to turn people's hearts from the clearly revealed Word of God. Various modern social movements and anti-scriptural religious organizations have been enlisted, wittingly or unwittingly, as part of the overall strategy to win control of the church.

Ours is a day when truth has been dragged to the scaffold and the great satanic lie of secular humanism has been exalted to the throne of understanding. Ours is a day when truth has been trampled under the heels of moral relativism, while satanic lies have been elevated profanely, even unto the very altars and pulpits of the holy Christian and apostolic church. Ours is a day when many preachers, schooled in liberal seminaries, have set aside the sacred writings of Scripture to proclaim the myths and fantasies of apostate, Satan-inspired theologies. Ours is a day when the gospel of the world's only Savior, Jesus Christ, has been set aside for the new doctrines of liberation theology, universalism, and moral relativism. Many sacred doctrines of the church have not only been set aside but are mocked and ridiculed as they are discarded.

How can we stand against such satanic attacks? Is it possible that God has brought his church into the latter part of the twentieth century only to have it die at the hands of Satan and his hordes? Never! We can stand today in the same power and certain hope that Jesus and all his great saints through the centuries knew and experienced. Like them, we too can have complete and total victory.

Let us then look together at Jesus' great battle with Satan. Let us look and learn. Let us look and be empowered in the same manner.

Matthew, chapter 4, presents one of the greatest scenes of combat in all of human history. This combat was not unique because of the technology of the armaments or the number of combatants. It was unique because the outcome of this battle would determine the destiny of the world and of every human being, including you and me.

Satan was truly prepared for this conflict with Jesus. His arsenal was ready. His arguments had been meticulously prepared and his strategy rehearsed. Jesus also was prepared. It was he who chose the weapon with which the battle would be fought. His was the most powerful weapon the world has ever seen. It dwarfs even our great nuclear arsenals of today. That weapon is the Word of God.

This great weapon of warfare, which Jesus so expertly used, is graciously given to us today by our heavenly Father. It worked for Jesus, for Luther, for Wesley and Moody, and it will do its work perfectly for you and me also. It never fails.

Years ago, the outspoken atheist Voltaire said, "Fifty years from now, the world will hear no more of the Bible." Ironically, the year he died, the British Museum paid $500,000 for an old copy of Scripture, while the first edition of Voltaire's works sold at a local bookstore for less than eight cents. His house was sold to the Geneva Bible Society.

God's Word is a personal Word. It is a practical Word, and it is a powerful Word. The Bible is a book of comfort. It is a book of hope. It is a book that may disturb you and shake you to the foundations. The beauty of Jesus is seen on every page. "*Sola Scriptura!*" Luther cried, "Scripture alone!" In the hands of Jesus, in the hands of Luther, or in your hands, it will always stand the test and produce the inevitable victory.

Surely Matthew 4 is written for our instruction. Jesus could have chosen and used many weapons. He might have responded by calling a legion of angels to trample Satan under foot. He could have been transfigured before that rascal and proved his divinity on the spot. But instead, Jesus, in his full humanity, to identify with you and me, chose to use the Word of God. This was his common practice. All through his earthly ministry, he spoke about and used the living Word of God. When he taught, he taught the Scriptures. When he shared about himself, his resurrection, and his coming again, he used the Scriptures. The Word of God was constantly on his lips. So it ought to be for us. "I have hidden your word in my heart . . ." (Ps. 119:11, NIV). "Your word is a lamp to my feet and a light for my path" (Ps. 119:105, NIV).

Jesus was led by the Spirit into the wilderness, and afterwards he was tempted by the devil. After fasting forty days and nights, Jesus was very hungry. At that moment, the tempter came to him and said, "If you are the Son of God, tell these stones to become bread." Note the timing of Satan. He knows when we are weak. He knows when we are most vulnerable. Satan loves that little word "if." He enjoys casting doubt.

Jesus had come to earth to identify with us. Had he used his true divinity for his own purpose, how would he be like us? "You have the power," Satan was telling Jesus. "Use it for yourself. Who will ever know?" How similar is Satan's message to us today! "If you are a Christian, why are you going through these trials just now? If you are a Christian and God is so loving, why does he permit these things to happen to you?"

Three times Satan approached Jesus, beginning his attack with his weapon—"if." And three times Jesus responded, "It is written." "It is written." "It is written." To the first temptation Jesus replied, "It is written: 'Man does not live on bread alone, but on every word that comes from the mouth of God.'" He was quoting Deuteronomy 8:3. Here was great demonstration of power, no elaborate argument. Jesus used the simple Word of God: "It is written."

Paul said to Timothy, "Do your best to present yourself to God as one approved, a workman who does not need to be ashamed and who correctly handles the word of truth" (2 Tim. 2:15, NIV). We today need to know the Word of God and have it at the ready for every situation. Concerning the third commandment, Martin Luther said, "Therefore, you must continually keep God's Word in your heart, on your lips and in your ears, for where the heart stands idle and the Word is not heard, the devil breaks in and does damage before we realize it."

"Many does not live on bread alone, but on *every* word that comes from the mouth of God." How important it is that we recognize that every word in the Scriptures is precious and every promise is for us! "It is written" is our infallible standard and our never-failing weapon of spiritual warfare today.

Satan does not know when to quit. He is a very persistent fellow. After losing round one with Jesus, he did not go away. Instead, he took Jesus to the Holy City and set him on the highest point of the temple, saying, "If you are the Son of God . . . throw yourself down. For it is written: 'He will command his angels concerning you, and they will lift you up in their hands, so that you will not strike your foot against a stone.'" Here the devil was quoting Psalm 91. Satan loves to quote Scripture and to misquote it as well. It was a battle of the texts. But then, as now, Scripture that is falsely interpreted and falsely used will never work.

The perversion of Scripture is one of Satan's best and most often used tactics. In 2 Timothy we read:

> The time will come when men will not put up with sound doctrine. Instead, to suit their own desires, they will gather around them a great number of teachers to say what their itching ears want to hear. They will turn their ears away from the truth and turn aside to myths [2 Tim. 4:3–4, NIV].

Such is happening today across the vast church. Satan has marched into the very structure of the church with his perversions of Scripture and his lies. But if church people really knew the Word of God and had it growing in their hearts, he would never get away with it. "My people are destroyed," says the Lord, "from lack of knowledge" (Hos. 4:6, NIV).

Those who espouse liberation theology or universalism and countenance sin within the church today are instruments of Satan. Such liberal theology is devoid of life and power. When is the last time you heard of people being born again after hearing such liberal, perverted teaching? When is the last time you saw revival breaking forth from a liberal pulpit? Never! And you never will.

One of the great men of God in this age is W. A. Criswell. He has upheld the Scriptures through his many years of ministry in the Southern Baptist Convention. Dr. Criswell said in his book *Why I Preach That the Bible Is Literally True*:

> The most important question for the religious world today is this, "Is the Bible the Word of God?" If the Bible is the Word of God, we have an absolutely trustworthy guide for all answers our soul desires to know. We have a starting point from whence we can proceed to the conquest of the whole realm of religious truth. We have an assurance of our salvation and the glories of the world to come. But if the Bible is not the Word of God, it is a mere product of man's speculation. If it is not altogether trustworthy in regard to religious and eternal truth, then we are all in a trackless wilderness, not knowing where to go or where to turn.[1]

I will continue his quote because it is so powerful and appropriate for us today.

> Truly there is not a sadder or more tragic sight than to look upon a minister or professor of divinity attacking or ridiculing the Word of God, the anchor of the human soul. There is a depth of hypocrisy about min-

---

1. W. A. Criswell, *Why I Preach That the Bible Is Literally True* (Nashville: Broadman, 1969), pp. 150–51.

isters attacking the Bible that is unusually heinous. We have public halls, houses of assemblies, scholastic academies and civic auditoriums where the Bible and Christianity may be assaulted without interruption. But to see a minister of the Gospel mount the pulpit to find fault with the Word of God and to decry it as revelation of the truth of heaven, is of all things most sad.[2]

Jesus' response to Satan's quoting Scripture was to use the Word of God rightly: "It is also written: 'Do not put the Lord your God to the test.'" Jesus believed it. He taught it. He demonstrated it. Those who misuse Scripture do well to remember that "God cannot be mocked" (Gal. 6:7, NIV).

Still Satan would not quit. His third and final assault brought Jesus to a very high mountain where he was shown all the kingdoms of the world in all their splendor. Satan said, "All this I will give you . . . if you will bow down and worship me." Quoting Deuteronomy 6:13, Jesus said to him, "Away from me, Satan! For it is written: 'Worship the Lord your God, and serve him only.'"

The final test, the tactic that so often works on so many, was compromise. "Give just a little." Satan with his lies promises us the sun, moon, and stars but delivers only pain, heartache, and shame. Jesus saw through his deceit, and so can we, in the power of the Holy Spirit.

"It is written" is our standard, too. If the devil brought out an army and unleashed every demon in hell against you, he could not defeat you, so long as you had the Word of God rightly flowing from your heart, for Satan cannot stand against the living Word of God. As Luther said, "One little Word shall fell him." The calm of Jesus' heart in the face of such a great and powerful enemy had its source in the sure hope of God's Word.

God the Holy Spirit has placed in the hands of all God's children this amazing and powerful weapon to fell the giant of the underworld. People said of Goliath's sword that there was none like it. Yet out on the field of battle, little David, with no more than a simple stone sent off in the power of God's Word, brought Goliath down and sent his legions fleeing.

Soldiers of Christ, arise! On this great Reformation Day, renew your commitment. Don your armor. The battle is the Lord's! Onward to reformation and victory now in the strength and power of his mighty, unchanging, inspired, infallible, and invincible Word!

Soli Deo Gloria! To God alone be glory!

2. Ibid.

23

A Widow's Mite or Might?
Kenneth M. Meyer

In His teaching He was saying: "Beware of the scribes who like to walk around in long robes, and like respectful greetings in the market places, and chief seats in the synagogues, and places of honor at banquets. They are the ones who devour widows' houses, and for appearance's sake offer long prayers; these will receive greater condemnation."

And He sat down opposite the treasury, and began observing how the multitude were putting money into the treasury; and many rich people were putting in large sums. And a poor widow came and put in two small copper coins, which amount to a cent. And calling His disciples to Him, He said to them, "Truly I say to you, this poor widow put in more than all the contributors to the treasury; for they all put in out of their surplus, but she, out of her poverty, put in all she owned, all she had to live on."

Mark 12:38–44 (NASB)

What an amazing experience! Jesus had just finished an extended teaching ministry and entered the temple area. His teaching did not end, however, for he now illustrated it from the temple offering. The Gospels tell us that he sat down and viewed the "treasury"—the place near the temple entrance where gifts and dues were deposited. Just think: Jesus watched the offering!

The parade of donors continued under Christ's eyes. Some of the rich were probably displaying large gifts ostentatiously, trying to attract all the attention they could. They were giving for show. Some may have wanted especially to impress this wise and popular teacher.

Then a widow, perhaps identifiable by her mourning dress, came

177

into the treasury area and unobtrusively dropped in two small *lepta*—coins now known as the "widow's mite" but worth less than one cent today. Jesus startled the disciples with his statement that this widow gave more than all the other donors combined, for while they gave out of their surplus, she gave all that she owned. Her gift was a great sacrifice.

Now we should not infer from this episode that Christ despises large gifts. Nor should we suppose that if we want to win his approval, we must give everything we have. Jesus did not imply either of these ideas. But this narrative does teach some basic principles about Christian stewardship that are applicable today. Let's see what they are.

Our Stewardship Does Not Go Unnoticed

Our stewardship does not go unnoticed. Mark 12:41 states this fact clearly: "He [Jesus] sat down . . . and began observing" the treasury.

A common notion among some believers is that there is a dichotomy between the material and spiritual. They reason that somehow our prayer life and Bible reading come under God' scrutiny, but not our checkbook.

Jesus exposed the error of this thinking when he deliberately and carefully observed the gifts that people were placing in the treasury. He still carries on this observation today. As Christian stewards, we must recognize that our spending habits, our money management, and our tithes and offerings are noticed by God. If we are eventually accountable for the "deeds [done] in the body," as Paul declares (2 Cor. 5:10, NASB), then why should we suppose that this accountability does not apply to our financial stewardship as well?

Jesus noted not only how much the people gave, but also the spirit and motivation behind their gifts. He saw that some of the rich gave to be seen, much like the scribes referred to in the preceding verses whom Jesus condemned for their ostentatious display of false piety (Mark 12:38–40). Many rich people were putting in large amounts, but the widow, "out of her poverty, put in all she owned." Jesus, knowing the human heart, saw that the motivation of the rich and that of the widow were worlds apart. The rich—even the most generous among them, and some were very generous, donating large sums—all gave out of their surplus, their financial leftovers. None of them—not even one—gave sacrificially. As he observed the donors deposit their gifts, Jesus quickly identified those whose giving was a mere show, staged for the benefit of their own pride by winning applause from others. By contrast, the widow, who sought to conceal her humble yet costly gift from all notice, was motivated by her love for God and her faith in his continuous provision.

Our stewardship is observed by God. He knows our heart, our bank account, and our motivation. Do we give to be noticed and praised by others? Do we give to compensate for our guilt? Or do we give, like this poor widow, to express our gratitude to God for all his goodness to us and our complete trust in his unfailing care in the future?

A renowned preacher followed the ushers down the aisle one Sunday, observing the offering of his parishioners. One can imagine the quandry of the congregation at this unorthodox behavior. When, a little later, he entered the pulpit, the preacher began his stewardship sermon by commenting on what he had done.

God does what that preacher did, only he does it *every* Sunday. Our stewardship does not go unobserved. We need to remember that.

Our Stewardship Does Not Go Unevaluated

We learn a second principle from this incident of the widow's mite. *Our stewardship does not go unevaluated.*

The verb for "cast" in verse 41 (KJV) is in the imperfect tense, implying that a stream of people were coming to the temple treasury and depositing their gifts, while Jesus watched them. He did not merely observe the people and their offerings, however. He also evaluated them.

After a while, Jesus called his disciples, who were nearby, over to him. There was a lesson in these offerings he didn't want the disciples to miss. He underlined its importance by introducing it with the emphatic term "truly" (v. 43). Now he shared with them his evaluation.

It may seem to us that Jesus knew very little about arithmetic. Mark tells us that he said that this pauper widow gave more than all the others. Be sure you understand Jesus' meaning. He didn't say that the widow contributed more than *any* of the other donors—some of whom made very large contributions. He said that this poor widow gave more than *all* the other donors combined.

Jesus' evaluation startles us because it is not based on the size of the gift. It is based on the giver's motivation and capability to give. The widow made the smallest offering Jesus saw that day. But to her the cost of that offering was very great indeed. In grateful, humble, loving devotion to God, she gave everything she had. All of the others gave out of their surplus, their leftovers. She gave all she had to live on. Her gift alone was a sacrifice.

This isn't the way we view contributions to the church today, is it? We laud the large contributions and give them prominence. Yet the millionaire's large gift may be surplus, while some other person's few dollars may be a sacrifice. God's work today seems more often to operate on the surplus of God's people than on their sacrifices.

In the Sermon on the Mount, Jesus gave further instructions on this subject of stewardship (Matt 6:1–4). There he warned that offerings given in a spirit of pride and for self-aggrandizement receive no recognition whatever from God. Our giving, like our praying, should be done "in secret." One of the largest gifts ever received by Trinity Evangelical Divinity School—not a surplus gift, but a sacrificial one—was given with the stipulation that the donor's name not be revealed.

The rich gave out of their wealth; the widow gave out of her extreme poverty. The motivation and the capability of the givers were quite different. The stewardship of the rich cost little; the stewardship of the widow cost everything.

A few years ago, during the Ethiopian famine, NBC News showed how various people responded to the crisis. A class of schoolchildren in the Harlem ghetto was asked to bring a penny each to help the starving, but not one child came with less than a dollar! One little boy went home and broke open his piggy bank and gave all eighteen dollars to help the famine victims. The dollars were insignificant; the motivation was magnificent.

Our stewardship does not go unevaluated. We need to remember that, too.

Our Stewardship Does Not Go Unappreciated

We learn one more principle from this story. *Our stewardship does not go unappreciated.*

The widow came to the temple to worship, and as an act of worship she brought her offering. Her stewardship did not go unnoticed or unevaluated, nor did it go unappreciated.

All of the essential elements in the term "stewardship" are found in this widow's gift. The element of faith was evident. Her faith was of the risk-taking kind, for the words of Jesus stress the fact that she gave every piece of money she owned. When she left the temple, she didn't have a cent to her name. She didn't know where her next meal would come from. She may have had children at home who depended on her for food and clothing and all the necessities of life. Yet she gave her entire livelihood to God, trusting him to provide for her and her family. Her faith was like that of the servant in Jesus' parable whose master entrusted him with the management of five talents (Matt. 24:14–21). He risked the five talents in a wise trading venture and was rewarded by his master.

Faithful Christian stewardship is an expression of the faith that trusts God to provide for every need of his servant. The gifts of the rich betrayed their false sense of security. They depended on themselves rather than on God.

The widow's gift also showed that she recognized her account-ability to God. The New Testament term for steward means "house manager," or a person who manages someone else's possessions for him. The widow knew that the little she had belonged to God and was held in trust for him. She had a keen awareness of her accountability to God for the use she made of the resources he had entrusted to her, however meager they might be.

Stewardship and accountability go hand in hand. If all that we have belongs to God and we are managers of it for him, then we are ac-countable to him for the use we make of his possessions. Someday we shall have to give account to him of our stewardship.

This poor widow did not come to the temple that day anticipating that she would be recorded in history for giving her humble gift to God. Very likely, she didn't think God would even notice her gift, much less commend her for it. Her offering was so small by ordinary human calculation, yet it did not go unappreciated by God. Though she never suspected it, Jesus honored her for her gift, emphasizing it in the Gos-pel story by making it the ideal for Christian giving throughout all the centuries to come. By giving her all to God, she showed she was one in spirit with him who only a few days later would give his all to God for the salvation of the world.

Faithful stewardship never goes unappreciated. That, too, we need to remember.

What is God's verdict on your stewardship? Does it show your rec-ognition that he is the rightful owner of all that you possess? Is your motivation pleasing to him?

Faithful stewardship, like that of the widow, transforms a mite into God's might.

24

Call to Mission
Mariano DiGangi

> In the church at Antioch there were prophets and teachers: Barnabas, Simeon called Niger, Lucius of Cyrene, Manaen (who had been brought up with Herod the tetrarch) and Saul. While they were worshiping the Lord and fasting, the Holy Spirit said, "Set apart for me Barnabas and Saul for the work to which I have called them." So after they had fasted and prayed, they placed their hands on them and sent them off. The two of them, sent on their way by the Holy Spirit, went down to Seleucia and sailed from there to Cyprus. When they arrived at Salamis, they proclaimed the word of God in the Jewish synagogues. John was with them as their helper.
>
> Acts 13:1–5 (NIV)

How would you define the mission of the church? Do you think that we should stick to the "simple gospel," saving souls for eternity while steering clear of the controversial social issues? Or do you suppose that since a loving God assures everyone of salvation, we should now concentrate on changing the structures of contemporary society along leftist lines? Or is mission meant only for an effete elite, an eccentric clique concerned with exotic places, determined to civilize and democratize lesser breeds? Do you consider the missionary movement as obsolete, a vestige of the colonial era, an instrument of cultural aggression?

To rediscover the mission of the church, we must get back to the Bible. Here, in God's written Word, we are given authentic revelation about the Lord's will for his people in the world. The Great Commandment concerning love to neighbor is amplified in the Great Commission. We express love to our neighbor not alone in healing the sick, feeding the hungry, teaching the unlearned, and sheltering the refugee, but in sharing the gospel and making disciples.

Here in Acts 13:1–5, we learn how one congregation heard and answered the Lord's call to mission:

> In the church at Antioch, there were prophets and teachers. . . . While they were worshiping the Lord and fasting, the Holy Spirit said, "Set apart for me Barnabas and Saul for the work to which I have called them." So after they had fasted and prayed, they placed their hands on them and sent them off. The two of them, sent on their way by the Holy Spirit, went down to Seleucia and sailed from there to Cyprus. When they arrived at Salamis, they proclaimed the word of God in the Jewish synagogues. John was with them as their helper [NIV].

This brief but significant narrative describes the first piece of planned "overseas mission" carried out by the representatives of a church, rather than by solitary individuals, and begun by a deliberate decision, inspired by the Spirit.

The Worship of the Lord

God's clear call to mission comes in the context of worship. Recall the story of Moses. At the sign of the burning bush—confronted with mystery, beholding flames of fire, standing on holy ground—Moses has a memorable encounter with the true and living God. Reverent in the presence of the Almighty, the God of Abraham, Isaac, and Jacob, Moses is summoned to a mission involving conflict with Pharaoh and the gods of Egypt—a mission of liberation for an oppressed people (Exod. 3:1–10).

Look at Isaiah in his moment of grief. King Uzziah, a most able and respected administrator, has died. Not even monarchs are immune to mortality. Isaiah goes to the temple with his anguish. Suddenly he sees the Lord enthroned and adored. As the seraphs worship him whose holiness is perfect and whose glory fills both heaven and earth, Isaiah is struck with stunning force by a sense of sin. Convicted of his iniquity, he confesses it in God's holy presence. Then does the mourning, penitent Isaiah receive the cleansing of divine grace and hear the call to go as the servant of a divine message. Grateful for the mercy that has taken away his guilt, Isaiah responds willingly to the commission of the

King of kings (Isa. 6:1–8). He is ready to be sent as a spokesman for God.

In the words of our text, Luke tells us of a worship situation at Syrian Antioch. That city was famous for its glamorous cosmopolitan character. Cultured, sophisticated, affluent, given to commerce and the pursuit of pleasure, it was exposed to the life-changing gospel when refugees for the cause of Christ shared the good news with anyone who cared to listen. Many turned to the Lord. Now, as the young church worships, the call to mission is heard. At Syrian Antioch, you had Barnabas, always generous and encouraging; Simeon from northern Africa; Lucius, a Cyrenian; Manaen, who had parted company with his foster brother Herod Antipas to follow the Master; and Saul of Tarsus, a persecutor of the saints transformed into a powerful preacher of the Savior. As they worshiped, the call came.

An Asian mission leader tells of a Christian convention at which the speaker was Sadhu Sundar Singh. The Lord had led him to focus on the spiritual needs of the Himalayan mountain kingdom of Nepal. A pregnant woman responded to Sundar Singh's impassioned appeal by dedicating her unborn child to the cause of Christ. That child, coming to manhood, became the first Indian missionary to Nepal.

Do we gather together out of mere formality, or is our time of worship vibrant with expectancy? Just about the only sense of expectancy many people have is that the preacher will be through in less than twenty minutes. We live in an era of sermonettes for Christianettes. When we meet in his name, however, we ought to be eager to hear what the Lord wants to tell us, his servants. Reverence in his presence prepares us for hearing the call to serve him.

Worship is not only the context of the call to mission, but is also the climax of the process of mission. This comes through very clearly in the last book of the Bible. There are those who think of Revelation as a grand crystal ball for the exclusive use of those with eschatological expertise. They abuse it as a stimulant to wild speculation and sectarian views. No wonder that the millennium may be defined as a thousand-year period of peace over which Christians fight! Let us never forget that the focal point of the Apocalypse is not the Antichrist but Jesus Christ. Here we see the Lamb, once slain for the sins of his people but now crowned with glory and honor. Hymns throughout this book praise the Lord of creation and redemption. The devout worship him who has set men free from the penalty and power of sin through the ransom price of personal sacrifice. He has redeemed them out of every tribe, language, people, and nation on the face of the earth, to serve as a royal priesthood in the presence of God (Rev. 5:9–14). The goal of mission is far more than the salvation of the individual, the growth of the church, or the healing of the nations. The ultimate goal of mission is nothing less than the worship of our Savior and Lord.

The Leadership of the Spirit

Mission did not originate in the fertile mind of someone looking for a project to absorb manpower and money. Mission flows from the very heart of God, who is not willing that any should perish but desires that all should come to repentance (2 Peter 3:9). It is the Spirit of God—the missionary Spirit—who provides both the direction and dynamic for the enterprise of love.

The Spirit gives direction. He requisitions Barnabas and Saul for the work of witness in the world. There is no doubt about the imperative mood in which the Spirit speaks. Mission is not an option, but an obligation demanding obedience. Failure to comply would be sin. A congregation that is not mission-minded is unspiritual. It is living in sin. Make no mistake about it. The Spirit summons the church to undertake the active evangelization of the pagan world. What is the Spirit telling us to do, as we see the constant influx of international students, migrants, and immigrants into our cities?

Barnabas had already been involved in generous giving for the support of the poor and warmhearted sponsorship for a new convert whose notorious past caused others to treat him with suspicion. Barnabas had also shown his skill in encouraging young believers to follow Christ faithfully, even though surrounded by a heathen atmosphere. Saul had not only experienced conviction and conversion, but received a commission from the Lord to open blind eyes, turn pagans from darkness to light, from the power of Satan to God, so that they could receive forgiveness of sins and a place among those who are sanctified through faith in Christ. Now Paul and Barnabas are to be set apart for mission in a new way.

How did the Spirit's call draw the congregation into the work of mission? Did he speak directly from heaven? Or was his voice heard through the prophets in the fellowship at Syrian Antioch? Did he make his will known as some of the teachers in that congregation expounded missionary texts like Genesis 12:1–3, Psalm 2:8, or Isaiah 52:7? Do we hear what the Spirit is saying to the churches today through the exposition of Scripture and the images of suffering on our television screens?

We know that the same Spirit who gives direction also grants the dynamic essential for the task. This is plainly taught in the gospel according to John. Our Lord's promises, recorded by that beloved disciple, make it abundantly clear that the power of the Spirit is never granted for mere private enjoyment or public display, but to enlighten and empower us so that we may serve him in the world. The Spirit guides us into an understanding of God's truth, revealed in the Scriptures. The Spirit comes alongside to support our witness to Christ, so that we can endure the indifference and hostility of the world. The Spirit convicts those who hear the Word and opens the way to eternal life (John 14:16–17; 15:26–27; 16:13–14; 20:21–22).

The Partnership of the Church

God's usual method is not to act directly from the sky, but to involve people like ourselves in fulfilling his plans. That is how the miracle of the incarnation came about. The Spirit caused Mary to conceive, and she showed obedient faith in the acceptance of God's will. That is how the inspired Scriptures were produced. Holy men of God spoke, but as they were moved by the Spirit's powerful impulse (2 Peter 1:21). That is how our sanctification becomes a reality. We work out our salvation in fear and trembling, yet knowing that God is at work in us to accomplish his purpose (Phil. 2:12–13).

Barnabas and Paul were sent not only by the Spirit, but also by the saints at Syrian Antioch: ". . . they sent them off. The two of them, sent on their way by the Holy Spirit, went down to Seleucia and sailed from there to Cyprus" (Acts 13:3–4, NIV). This partnership of the church is seen in several ways: listening, fasting, praying, associating, and sending. Let us consider each of these in turn.

Listening. The congregation at Antioch heard what the Spirit said. Do we hear what the Spirit is saying to our churches today? Some churches are closed to his voice because they are infected with the virus of universalism and reason that if God is love, and only love, then no one will ever be lost. Why bother to urge people to repent and believe the gospel, if they are already destined to salvation?

Others fail to hear the Spirit because of syncretism. Their position is that dialogue with the adherents of other faiths is fine, but you must not press the claims of Christ as the only Savior and Judge or call anyone to decision. After all, they say, there's some truth in every religion. Why challenge others to choose Christ?

The biggest barrier to hearing the Spirit's call, however, is not universalism or syncretism, but parochialism. When congregations become so preoccupied with their own comfort, overconcerned about their own mortgages, and absorbed in their own conflicts, they cannot hear what the Spirit is saying to them. The disciples at Syrian Antioch, however, listened when the Spirit spoke. So must we.

Fasting. Surely the congregation described by Luke did not fast as a fleeting dietary fad, nor as a means to atone for sin and acquire merit. If they fasted in Syrian Antioch, it was for the furtherance of mission. Fasting not only released time for prayer but also provided funds for the support of the Lord's work in the world.

I was privileged to participate in the great Lausanne Congress for World Evangelization, which drew Christian leadership from no less than 150 nations. We agreed to fast for an entire day and donate what would have been spent on our food to relieve world hunger. At the great mission convention sponsored by the InterVarsity Christian Fellowship on the Urbana campus of the University of Illinois, thousands of students have done the same. I have also seen figurative fasting in the gracious action of a schoolteacher who gave up what she had saved for a trip around the world so that a pioneer program of Christian literature could be funded for Africa.

In Victorian England, many mission-minded people joined a "Do Without" Society, in order to release money for the furtherance of the gospel. Would we qualify to join that group today? What are we willing to deny ourselves to make missionary advance possible in our time?

Praying. The supportive fellowship at Syrian Antioch prayed for those who were about to embark on a history-making journey destined to change the face of Europe. We know that Paul valued the intercession of other disciples as he engaged in disciple making. He assured the Corinthians that their prayers really helped, and that God had brought blessing to many in answer to their prayers (2 Cor. 1:11). Paul urged the Romans to join him in his spiritual struggle by praying to God for him (Rom. 15:30). He asked the Colossians to intercede, that doors might open for the entry of the gospel and he might proclaim Christ with clarity (Col. 4:3–4). Paul also encouraged the Thessalonians to pray that the gospel message might be spread widely and received warmly (2 Thess. 3:1).

The truth, as Alan Redpath reminds us, is this:

> . . . nobody should ever go to the field for God, or to any service for God, alone. He must have those who will pray, who are with him in spirit at his side constantly, for the man who goes in answer to God's call will face many shattering disillusionments. He will be subjected to perils he has never before experienced. He will be submitted [sic] to temptations hitherto unknown. He will have to face loneliness that he had never imagined, and homesickness. . . . But that man who has left everything in life which he might hold dear is entitled to spiritual protection and to expect it from men who know how to pray and to write, and above all who know how to enter into his needs and share them at the throne of grace.

The men and women who respond to Christ's call through mission service are not super-saints exempt from physical ills, emotional stress, or spiritual struggle. Think of your own needs, remember theirs, and pray for them.

Associating. We are told that hands were laid on Barnabas and Paul. Why was this done? Did they suppose that some magical power would be conferred on them by this ritual? Not at all. By this tangible and visible expression, the congregation at Syrian Antioch symbolized its relationship to the missionaries. Paul and Barnabas were going as ambassadors of Christ the King, bearing a message of reconciliation to an alienated world. But they were also going as representatives of that supportive fellowship. They would go where other members of the congregation could not. Through their faithful witness and loving service, the Christian community of Syrian Antioch would reach out to people in need far beyond its city limits. Do we consider missionaries as an extension of the local church? Or do we simply regard them as employees of some mission agency that is related to the church only financially?

Sending. Who actually sends the missionary to serve the people in Peru or Pakistan? Is it the mission agency, denominational or transdenominational? Scripture gives us a very definite answer. The sending is done by the Son, the Spirit, and the saints (Matt. 9:38; Acts 13:3–4), but we must not overlook the importance of the local church in the sending process. A mission agency serves as the channel between needs "over there" and resources "back home." It has functional expertise, supervises orientation and language training and placement, provides for pastoral care, arranges for deputation and continuing education on home leave, and helps in the process of reentry when the period of service is over. Not too many congregations are equipped to do all this. But without the local church, where would mission boards recruit candidates and receive support in terms of prayer and giving?

Congregations need to be more deeply involved in candidate recruitment. Along with nurturing believers and expanding their horizons for service and witness, they should also discern and develop gifts. Churches should, moreover, recommend individuals to mission agencies for consideration as potential personnel.

One of the most encouraging trends in this half of the twentieth century is the growing involvement of Third World churches in sending forth servants of the gospel. A country like Korea, with more than nine thousand students in Bible colleges, has provided nearly one thousand missionaries. India now has more than one hundred indigenous mission organizations and three thousand men and women sharing in the spread of the gospel. Brazil is another nation whose churches have a great potential for sending out large numbers of missionaries. But let us never forget that billions of people on this planet have yet to hear the message of God's grace in Jesus Christ. This should be an incentive to plead with the Lord of the harvest, that he may send forth more laborers into his harvest field (Matt. 9:38).

The Stewardship of the Word

Luke's account mentions not only the worship of the Lord, the leadership of the Spirit, and the partnership of the church, but also the stewardship of the Word in connection with mission. This stewardship involves both presence and proclamation.

Presence. Paul and Barnabas did not operate by remote control, but actually went to the people they wanted to reach. They journeyed to the seaport city of Seleucia and sailed to Cyprus. That large island in the eastern end of the Mediterranean was home country for Barnabas. He knew its rugged mountains and fertile valleys. He knew something of its language, culture, and religion. Together with Paul, he went to Salamis and made contact with those who attended its synagogues. These would include both Jews who expected the coming of the promised Messiah and Gentiles looking for something better than pagan idolatry and immorality. Paul and Barnabas went to them, met with them, and spent time with them. Compassionate service and faithful witness still demand such presence.

Proclamation. Christ's servants were not only present, but articulate. As God in his providence gave them opportunity, they proclaimed the Word in the synagogues to Jews and Gentiles. In Lystra, later on, they would be speaking to people who knew nothing of the Scriptures but were aware of nature's changing seasons. At Athens, the audience would consist of Stoics and Epicureans interested in philosophy and poetry. In each instance, the starting point would be appropriate to the local situation. There was no stereotyped approach. Effective witness begins with people where they are. On Cyprus, at Salamis, in the synagogues, the missionaries proclaimed the Word of God. The proclamation of the Word means the presentation of the incarnate Word, Jesus Christ. We preach Christ, the God-man who died for the sins of his people and defeated death by resurrection on the third day after the crucifixion. Our preaching of the Word-made-flesh is based on the written Word, the Scriptures given by inspiration of God to serve as the infallible standard of belief and behavior. Here we face the moral law that shatters presumption and convicts of sin. Here we are offered the gospel of grace that brings forgiveness and new life to all who repent and believe.

Through preaching, literature, music, drama, radio, film, television, and visitation, it is our responsibility to present the incarnate Word, from the written Word, in the power of the Holy Spirit. Beyond all doubt, mission consists in far more than the delivery of a message through whatever medium is appropriate and available. "Religion that God our Father accepts as pure and faultless is this: to look after orphans and widows in their distress and to keep oneself from being polluted by the world" (James 1:27, NIV). But pursuit of personal piety and works of charity are not a valid substitute for the proclamation of the Word.

We rejoice over the fact that an estimated 78,000 people are added to the Christian population of this planet each day. Every week, about 1,000 new churches are established in Africa and Asia alone. There has been phenomenal growth among Protestants in Latin America. At the start of this century, they may have numbered only 50,000. By the year 2000, should present trends continue, there will be at least 100,000,000. But none of these facts and projections should lead us to pride or complacency. What of the almost three billion people who have yet to hear the gospel or have resisted Christ? The situation calls for far more than debate over the fate of "the unevangelized heathen." It demands obedience to the One whose claim and commission are unchanging: "All authority in heaven and on earth has been given to me. Therefore go and make disciples of all nations, baptizing them in the name of the Father and of the Son and of the Holy Spirit, and teaching them to obey everything I have commanded you. And surely I am with you always, to the very end of the age" (Matt. 28:18–20, NIV).

Challenged afresh by this assignment, and encouraged by the assurance of the Lord's presence, let us resolve to do his will by the fidelity of our witness and the integrity of our lives.

25

Give Yourself a Gratitude Gift
Neil B. Wiseman

In every thing give thanks: for this is the will of God in Christ Jesus concerning you.

1 Thessalonians 5:18 (KJV)

Give yourself a little gift today," suggests the clever sign in Aunt Sally Goggan's card shop.

At first, the idea sounds selfish, but it is done every day. Folks give themselves cars, homes, and Caribbean cruises. Expensive presents like pleasure, power, and profit appear on the gift lists of some individuals. Others give themselves miserable presents like broken marriages, bankrupt morals, undisciplined children, and addiction to drugs, food, or alcohol. But to give yourself a gift of gratitude should be carefully considered in light of the magnificent possibilities.

Thanksgiving—what a beautiful idea and what a noble emotion! Even though giving makes up one-half of the word *thanksgiving,* our mental picture of this annual celebration nearly shoves gratitude out of our thoughts. Since "more is better," Thanksgiving often focuses on abundant harvest, increased national product, full employment, plus a table burdened down by a bronzed turkey and pumpkin pies.

Calories by the thousands dance in our heads and settle on our middles. On Thanksgiving morning, families gather around their TV's to watch football games and Macy's pre-Christmas parade, while everyone anticipates the coming feast. Every year, near the end of November, Americans join to celebrate this holiday of national pride and family togetherness. Sometimes they even salt a bit of sentimental religious feeling into the day's activities.

In spite of our many other Thanksgiving traditions, the horn of plenty—the cornucopia—symbolizes what Thanksgiving mostly means.

But things may be changing. The consumer binge could be over. Pressing social issues impact the land. In a thousand different ways, the abandonment of personal piety takes its toll. Abused children, drug-burned-out teenagers, multiple-married young adults, and bored golden-agers are part of this landscape of frightening change. Apparently the Scriptures are accurate—life is more than food, drink, and pleasure (Matt. 6:25).

Changing circumstances and shifting culture did not affect the apostle Paul's thinking about gratitude. Evidently he believed you can persevere for God in all situations. He advises, "Be joyful always; pray continually; give thanks in all circumstances, for this is God's will for you in Christ Jesus" (1 Thess. 5:16–18, NIV). Paul's extravagances sound like overstatements. Be joyful *always*. Pray *continually*. Give thanks *in all circumstances*. Could he be serious?

Our Pilgrim forebears knew Paul was right when, in the midst of want, they met to express gratitude. And in 1863, in the midst of the war between the states, Abraham Lincoln wrote: "In the midst of a Civil War of unequal magnitude and severity . . . I invite my fellow citizens in every part of the United States to set aside and observe the last Thursday of November next as a day of thanksgiving and praise to our beneficent Father." In spite of circumstances, gratitude affirms faith.

Maybe this is a ripe time to give yourself a gift of gratitude. There are three things this self-gift will do.

Gratitude Mutes Our Arrogance

Sunny days and mountain peaks tend to encourage foolish pride. When things go well, it is easy to believe the myth about our independence. Steady employment, good health, money in the bank, and a fine education contribute to our idea that everything we possess comes from our applied brilliance or our hard work. Sophisticated self-sufficiency is part of the modern mind-set. Ideas of male macho and female rights tilt our thinking away from humility and reliance on God.

But Jesus' question after the healing of the ten lepers—"Where are the nine?" (Luke 17:17)—presses us, too. Too soon, almost immediately, all but one of the healed men forgot their physical pain and social isolation. Maybe they thought they were worthy of healing. They might have excused themselves by thinking that public praise to God was embarrassing, and so they would be thankful in more quiet ways. Or maybe they planned to thank God in their routine times of public worship. Perhaps they had to catch up on all the things they thought they needed to do. This eternally contemporary question judges every generation.

This Bible gratitude lesson is both powerful and personal. As long as we can jog, walk, or move, it is difficult to be thankful for these simple blessings. Yet, sad but true, one stabbing pain in the lower back or one cancer threat turns a person in utter dependence and heartfelt thanksgiving to the Savior for his provision.

To reflect on the percentages in the leper story provides an antidote for pride. Only one in ten returned to give thanks. The numbers sound accurate when you think about human nature. One in ten, or a hundred in a thousand—that is probably about the amount of gratitude you might expect from any group.

But make it personal. Compared to my blessings, my gratitude probably hovers around the 10 percent mark. And how does your gratitude compare to the blessings of your life? A self-gift of thanks raises the percentages.

Arrogance and pride are actually self-delusions. All of us have heard of the farmer who, when reminded of his partnership with God, said, "You should have seen this farm when God had it all by himself." We chuckle at the story because we know that God never farms an acreage without the help of a man. But there is another factor. Without God, the farmer has no land, no seed, no rain, and no energy to work. What human can accurately boast that he makes the sun, the soil, and the shower produce the golden grain? Or, to use Governor William Bradford's idea, who really believes he is personally responsible for protection from the ravages of savages, pestilence, and disease?

Gratitude produces in us a realistic dependence on divine resources. All we are and all we have has been given to us by God. Even as Jesus responded to the returning leper, he says to us in our times of gratitude, "Your faith has made you well" (Luke 17:19). Thanksgiving brings realism to the mind of the thanks-giver and ridicules our pride.

But there is a reverse kind of arrogance called self-pity. Gratitude provides a reality test for this self-imposed delusion, too. In the dentist's waiting room, two elderly women talked in the loud stage whisper caused by their hearing impairment. One told the other how lonely her life had been for several years while she lived alone after her husband's death. She admitted limitations because of her fixed income. But in the recent past she experienced a change. She met a rich gentleman. He bought her an expensive fur coat. He offered to send a chauffeur-driven limousine to pick her up for dinner. Obviously he had a meaningful relationship in mind. Still, two problems concerned her. She reasoned that he might not like her once he knew she resided in a mobile home; she did not want him to know her situation. Then, too, the man was stone deaf and a little arthritic. She faced a dilemma. Should she be grateful for his interest, his generosity, and his companionship? Or should she regret that he was so hard of hearing that they could never enjoy a conversation? Self-pity dominated her thoughts because of her limited circumstances. And she fretted about a future when she might have to care for a "crippled old dummy." She chose self-pity for what she did not possess in place of gratitude for what she already had.

Life is like that. Every pain has the potential for gratitude. Every problem provides an opportunity for stronger faith and new relationships. The need for surgery can make us dread the pain or thank God for the surgeon's skills. Rebellious children can cause us to curse the day the child was born or thank God for the good days of childhood and the possibility of better days ahead. Stormy weather can create dreary complaints or gratitude for the sunny days. The death of a spouse can produce a terror of the future or a song of thanksgiving for ten thousand shared joys. A broken souvenir can bring anger against the person who accidentally broke the object or a thought of thanks for all the times it produced a joyous memory. A thankful heart discovers blessings in what others overlook.

The idea is explained by Henry Ward Beecher, the great preacher: "Pride slays thanksgiving, but a humble mind is the soil out of which thanks naturally grow. A proud man is seldom a grateful man, for he never thinks he gets as much as he deserves."

Thanksgiving shows arrogance to be a spiritual fraud. So a self-gratitude gift moves the focus of our thoughts from self-sufficiency to God's abundance. True gratitude mutes arrogance—both the self-pity and the pride varieties. Thanksgiving is our declaration of dependence.

Gratitude Motivates Our Actions

Paul puts gratitude and thanks-living together, "Whatever you do, whether in word or deed, do it all in the name of the Lord Jesus, giving thanks to God the Father through him" (Col. 3:17, NIV). For Paul, thanksgiving, word, and deed all impact each other.

To our question, "How can I say thanks?" the Bible answers, "Show your gratitude in helpful deeds for God to your fellow human beings."

True thanks pushes us to action.

In this day of the fast buck and the easy deal, the idea of work has fallen on hard times. So, for some people, service to Christ has become a thing of the past. Others have lessened their activities and taken back part of their Christian commitments. But true thanksgiving is action, and gratitude leads us to servanthood.

We say thanks for life by living it fully and joyously in the way the Lord wants it lived. As each day begins, we open ourselves to his purposes with thanks for life and a request that we may be directed to share energy and love with someone who needs us.

Every God-given ability has some useful expression in the lives of other people. Every church needs more singers, more teachers, more intercessors, more givers, and more encouragers. No grateful person will use these abilities for his or her own purposes without also seeking to use them in the service of God. We say thanks for talents by using them.

We say thanks for health and happiness by ministry. Someone in the hospital needs our visit. A person who lives alone and dwells only on the memories of a thousand yesterdays needs to receive our note of encouragement. Someone who is shut in by illness needs a phone call. Even our own minor ailments fade in the light of being exposed to the deeper needs of other people.

Kingdom investments provide a channel for thankful action. Our faithful tithing helps make our churches strong. The remaining 90 percent is also considered a sacred trust from God. The Bible principle is accurate: where a man places his financial resources, there you will find his heart (Matt. 6:21).

We say thanks for persons who have contributed to our spiritual journey by making a similar impact on the weak and the young. By our kindness and love, little children are influenced in the development of their faith. Unbelievers, even the loud and tough kind, are shaped by a kind word and a Christian deed at a needed moment. People shape people. God works through people to affect people.

For the depressed, one psychiatrist prescribes a simple cure to be used for six weeks. He instructs his patients to say "Thank you" whenever anyone does them a favor and to emphasize the words with a smile. He receives a common reply, "But, doctor, no one ever does anything for me." The doctor says, "That's why you are sick, because you don't look for reasons to be thankful." Two results flow from his treatment: the patient becomes less discouraged, and persons who associate with the patient become more active in their affirming words and deeds toward the patient. Everyone is helped in the process. This treatment is a principle of life. Thanks given turn into appreciation received—a boomerang called gratitude.

Unique forces flow into and out of the life of a grateful Christian. Praise changes folks because it is hard to sing and complain at the same time. A thankful word lifts the spirit of both speaker and receiver. One more accurately sees events when looking through grateful eyes. The impact of praise is beyond measure. A word of thanks for the food changes the atmosphere of a meal. A word of gratitude for a kindly deed blesses the giver. A word of appreciation for a beautiful day changes a frown to a smile. An expression of thanks significantly impacts both the interior and the exterior dimensions of human experience.

The renowned mathematician Albert Einstein once wrote: "Many times a day I realize how much my own inner and outer life is built upon the labors of my fellowmen both living and dead, and how earnestly I must exert myself in order to give in return as much as I have received. All truly noble people are conscious of their indebtedness." It is true.

Every genuinely thankful Christian is an active servant of Christ. He cannot say thanks without giving. A self-gift of gratitude motivates our actions and affects other people.

Gratitude Multiplies Our Adoration

The cornerstone of worship is "Thanks be unto God for his unspeakable gift" (2 Cor. 9:15, KJV). The gift of grace in Jesus Christ is the starting point of our gratitude. Our profound appreciation to God includes a testimony from Scripture: "Old things are passed away; behold, all things are become new" (2 Cor. 5:17, KJV). Because of the Lord's miraculous work in our lives, we walk in wonder.

But it is easy to forget. One of Beethoven's pianos is housed in a Vienna museum. Before the surprised guard could stop her, on a whim a thoughtless teenager began to play "Chopsticks" on the famous instrument. Then she inquired, "What do other musicians think about this piano?" The attendant informed her that Paderewski had once visited this gallery. So she inquired, "Did he play something beautiful?" The guard replied, "No, no, Mr. Paderewski felt unworthy of even touching it." So it may be with us. In the presence of heavenly royalty, we can easily forget the King's warmth, be blind to his beauty, and be ·deaf to his music.

A preacher of an earlier era explained the vital relationship between gratitude and adoration: "Our thanks should be as fervent for mercies received, as our petitions for mercies sought." Thanksgiving restores the awe, the amazement, and the worship.

Adoration grows when we follow the songwriter's guidance: "Count your blessings, name them one by one, . . . Count your many blessings and it will surprise you what the Lord has done." When you count your blessings, you find them countless. Our main reason for gratitude is not "things," but God himself. By way of contrast, imagine a wealthy young man who comes to court a beautiful woman. After showering her with attention and gifts, he proposes marriage. Surely we would question her motives if she replied, "I want to marry you because I like what you can do for me. Your money will buy me lots of things. I like what you give me, but I am bored with you." We believers worship the Giver rather than the gift.

Check your thanksgiving list. Does it include the productive field as a witness of God's sustaining care? Does it list the love that adds meaning to all the relationships of your home, relatives, friends, and the church? Does it speak of worth in work, so you find strength to toil and a sense of achievement in your occupation? Does it place at the top the provision of Jesus for you, so his birth, death, and resurrection are the meaningful realities of your life? As you and I think thanks, the gratitude list grows.

Adoration and awe increase as we measure the quality of our life against what it would have been without God. God's gracious provisions are free to us and costly to him. His giving is abundant and continuous, and his gifts are available to all and abundantly worth having. As one family gathered around the heavy Thanksgiving table, the father prayed, "God, please add one more blessing—a thankful heart." We need that blessing, too.

Trudy, the cat of the comics, says he is thankful that he is not the turkey. Adoration grows when we consider what we have been spared. As he led his people in worship on a cold, rainy day, James Stalker, the Scottish preacher, prayed: "We thank Thee, O Lord, that not every day is like this." One simple believer often testified, "The Lord has been partial to me all my life." God's pleasant providences remind us of the pain and the problems we have missed. His ways are good.

God is a spendthrift. Redemption, mercy, abundance, protection, and grace are ours in magnificent supply. Gratitude produces emotions of wonder and worship.

Years ago, the *Sunday School Times* ran a story about a joyful Christian woman who was asked about her secret of happiness. She attributed it all to her "Thanks Book." She kept a simple journal in which she made daily entries like these:

"Saw a beautiful sunset."
"Talked to an inquisitive child."
"Received a compliment from my husband."
"Enjoyed a beautiful flower."
"Watched dancing flames in the fireplace."
"Rejoiced in the witness of a new convert."
"Heard the prayers of a saint."
"Gave a missionary offering."
"Thanked God for a good doctor."
"Had enough to eat."

A "Thanks Book"—either in an actual notebook or in a grateful heart—makes us sing with the Psalmist, "Bless the LORD, O my soul, and forget not all his benefits" (Ps. 103:2, KJV).

True gratitude causes us to remember all his benefits and gifts. So it includes thanks for past blessings, appreciation for present favors, and praise for promised grace. Our gratitude mutes arrogance, motivates actions, and multiplies adoration.

As a boy, Benjamin Franklin saw his father daily take their meat from the salt barrel. His father always prayed, "We thank Thee, Father, for the meat Thou hast provided." One day, young Franklin offered a suggestion: "Father, why not say one prayer over the whole barrel? Then you won't have to thank the Lord for every piece of meat." We are like that. We dump 364 days of blessing into a barrel and then remember our thanksgiving on but one day each year. Better that we have 364 days of thankfulness and save one day for the familiar pastime of complaining. *Give yourself a gift of gratitude*!

26

God's Word Is Our Great Heritage

Robert David Preus

> *But continue thou in the things which thou hast learned and hast been assured of, knowing of whom thou hast learned them; And that from a child thou hast known the holy scriptures, which are able to make thee wise unto salvation through faith which is in Christ Jesus. All scripture is given by inspiration of God, and is profitable for doctrine, for reproof, for correction, for instruction in righteousness: That the man of God may be perfect, thoroughly furnished unto all good works.*
>
> 2 Timothy 3:14–17 (KJV).

In our day of virtually worldwide revolution and insecurity, the most abiding thing you and I can possess and the most important legacy we can leave our children is knowledge. By excessive taxation or by simple confiscation, every material thing we own can be taken from us: our income, our capital, our wealth, even our property. This is actually happening all over the world today. The last thing that can be taken from us is what we have in our heads. If we know something, we can usually make a way for ourselves under difficult circumstances and can at least survive. And the more we know, the better our lives will be. It was a wise man, wise also in the ways of the world, who said, "Wisdom is the principal thing; therefore get wisdom: and with all thy getting get understanding" (Prov. 4:7, KJV).

Knowledge not only prepares us for our brief life here on earth. There is a higher knowledge, which opens doors of eternal life to us.

This is the knowledge of Jesus Christ. "And this is life eternal," he prays, "that they might know thee the only true God, and Jesus Christ, whom thou hast sent" (John 17:3, KJV). What does it mean to "know" Jesus Christ? It means not merely that I have a few facts at hand concerning his life and death. It means not merely that I regard him as a great teacher, a martyr, an example, or even the One who has revealed God's love to me. To know Christ means to know his benefits, to know what he has done for me. To know him means to say to him, "*my* Lord," "*my* God," "*my* Savior."

Where do we gain this knowledge that leads to eternal life? How do we learn to know Jesus Christ? How may we learn to recognize and appreciate the communion with God, the forgiveness, and the sure hope of eternal life, all of which are to be had only through him? The answer is simple and clear: through his Word. Just as Christ himself is life and light, the words he has spoken are spirit and life (John 6:63). Just as he is the foundation for our life with God, his Word is the foundation for our knowledge of this life in God. This Word through which we believe in him is, as he has said (John 17:20), the word of the apostles and prophets, the word of Holy Scripture. In keeping with this observance of Bible Sunday, I want to speak to you on the subject of the Scriptures and how precious they are to us all.

Scripture makes many statements and claims about itself, about its power, its authority, its divine origin. Most of these statements are brief and made only in passing. Of all such statements, our text today is the longest, the clearest, and the most complete. It offers three reasons why the Bible is a most precious treasure to every Christian: its power, its divine origin, and its practicality.

The Bible Is Powerful

In the opening words of our text, Paul is urging Timothy to hold fast and continue in everything that Paul has taught him. The apostle reminds his younger co-worker that everything he has taught him was taken from the Scriptures, the same Scriptures that Timothy learned as a child from his devout mother and grandmother. Why is it so paramount that Timothy continue faithfully in the doctrine of Scripture? Is it simply to remain loyal to cultural heritage? Or to remain well informed concerning God and his people and their history? No, Paul says, there is an infinitely more important reason. Scripture is power; it is "able to make thee wise unto salvation through faith which is in Christ Jesus."

Just what is this power that Scripture possesses? In the Middle Ages, certain monks would strap a Bible to their backs, thinking it would protect them wherever they went and ward off evil spirits. Ironically, some of these monks never even knew how to read. But this is making the Bible a fetish and its power something magical.

Today many scholars tell us that the Bible is unique in that it is the first and original witness to Christ and therein lies its power. But surely there is more to be said than that. We do not venerate the Bible simply because it is old. No, the power of Scripture is in its message. And its message is Christ. He is the essence, soul, and center of Scripture. As Luther used to say, "Christ is involved in Scripture through and through, like a body in its clothes." Scripture teaches; it makes us wise by teaching Christ crucified and placarding him before our eyes. For every penitent sinner this is a message of sweetest comfort. It can fill the most despondent, wretched heart with peace and joy and hope. For it tells every poor sinner of a Savior crucified and risen, a Savior God who thrusts himself into our sin, our misery, our death and hell, and takes our place, and then offers us forgiveness, reconciliation with God, righteousness, and salvation.

When we embrace this message of Scripture, we become wise. Not just because we have acquired a little more factual knowledge. Paul tells us that this message of Scripture comes to us "not . . . in word only, but also in power, and in the Holy Ghost, and in much assurance" (1 Thess. 1:5, KJV). It is God's power unto salvation. It not only informs us but seizes us and changes us and makes us a new creation, children of God. Therefore, you must never forget these words of our text or minimize them. The Scriptures are able—they have the inherent power, the very power of God—to make us wise unto salvation by bringing us to faith in Christ.

We must understand the full implication of this. Scripture is not merely like a billboard that speaks *about* Christ and eternal life. It *brings* Christ to us and in turn brings us poor, lost, dead sinners to Christ. What the living Word of Scripture has done in us is no less than what the living Word of Christ accomplished in dead Lazarus. It has given us life. So there is good reason for us to sing that old Lutheran hymn:

> Speak, O Lord, Thy servant heareth,
> To Thy word I now give heed;
> Life and Spirit Thy Word beareth,
> All Thy Word is truth indeed;

Death's dread power in me is rife;
Jesus, may thy Word of life
Fill my soul with love's strong fervor,
That I cling to Thee forever.

The Bible Is a Divine Word

Perhaps you are asking, "How can Scripture, a book, be so powerful?" Paul in our text seems to anticipate this question and, in giving an answer, he offers a second reason why we should highly treasure Scripture. "All Scripture is given by inspiration of God. . . ." Here Paul tells us that Scripture is not the product of men. It is not the result of human ingenuity or thought or decision, even though men obviously did the writing, consciously and willingly. No, Scripture is God's breath, God's utterance. It came forth from God's mouth, God's heart and will. It is not a hodgepodge that reflects the theology of Isaiah and Paul and James. It teaches *one* theology, the theology of God, and it reflects the divine mind and will.

Many theologians are telling us today that God is not the Author of the Bible but only of the lives of the human beings who wrote the Bible. But Paul says "No" to this. He does not even mention the human authors of Scripture, although he was one of them. He simply tells us that the Scriptures were breathed from God. Luther, therefore, is perfectly right when he says, "You are so to deal with Scripture that you bear in mind that God Himself is speaking to you."

The Bible is powerful to work faith in us and make us wise unto salvation because it is *God's* Word. What a tragedy, then, what a stupid and utter tragedy, ever to toss this Book of books into a corner and leave it to gather dust. On the other hand, what a joy and comfort to know that whenever you take it up to read it, whenever you hear it preached, whenever you meditate upon it, God himself is present— speaking to you and mediating to you his Son, his Holy Spirit, his forgiveness, and all the riches of his grace. And why should this not be a joy and comfort to us? You and I, living in this fallen, cursed, confused world where all people are liars, can have the confidence, even though we never see God, that he nevertheless speaks to us in the Bible. He speaks to us as directly and personally with the same truth and power as he spoke to Adam in the Garden of Eden and to Abraham on the fields of Mamre. Moses, who talked with God face to face, and the disciples, who daily sat at Jesus' feet and heard his words of eternal life, had no advantage over us. Do you see now what it means when we say that the Bible is God's Word?

The Bible Is Practical

The third reason why the Bible is such a treasure to every Christian is that it is eminently practical. Because the Bible is produced by the breath of God, because it is his Word, Paul says it is useful, "profitable"—profitable for four things. First, for doctrine—the Bible teaches a person the Christian faith. Second, for reproof—the Scriptures convince the man of God, they persuade him of the truth. Third, for correction—the Bible helps us to revise and amend our wrong ideas and lives. Fourth, for instruction in righteousness—the Scriptures train us, educate us in the way we should walk as men and women of God. In short, Paul tells us that in the Bible, God teaches us children of his all that we are to believe and do.

Notice that Paul also says that Scripture makes the man of God "... perfect." It makes every man of God fully equipped in every direction, fully prepared for every exigency of life and death, fully informed. Nothing else is mentioned. When you are instructed by Scripture, you are completely fitted for the Christian life. Think of that! Paul uses the strongest possible words, and he piles up words: "perfect, thoroughly furnished unto all good works."

What the apostle is trying to tell us here is simply this: the Bible is the most practical book in the world. God has made it the Book for all ages and all nations. It commends itself to every intellectual capacity, to every cultural setting, and for every human necessity. It sets forth its spiritual truth and saving doctrine to all people, great and small, learned and simple, good and bad; and all people can understand it and embrace it and love it and live in it.

Yet how we neglect and abuse this Word! How we waste our precious time on other things! In his day King Solomon could already say, "Of making many books there is no end" (Eccles. 12:12, KJV). How much more can this be said of our day! But most of these books are no good. They are either inane, or they cater to our baser instincts, or they seek to lead us astray.

But out of this tragic welter of darkness, the Bible still shines bright and clear. It not only informs us how to be a good husband or wife, a good parent, a good citizen. It not only teaches us good business principles, good morals, good taste. It gives us a new outlook on life, a heavenly viewpoint, which no other book in the world can give. It sets us on the way toward eternal life, and the way of faith in Christ.

The Bible brings God to us; it brings heaven to earth; it brings hope to our confusion and grace into our life of sin and sorrow. It tells us the thoughts of God, his thoughts of peace toward us and not of evil. It reveals the hidden and deep things of God's glory and grace. It is the Lord's staff, which comforts us in every trouble and distress. It is our spiritual meat and drink, which nourishes and strengthens us every day of our lives. And greatest of all, it unites us with our Savior. So we sing in doxology:

> Lord, Thy words are waters living,
> Where I quench my thirsty need;
> Lord, Thy words are breath life-giving;
> On Thy words my soul doth feed;
> Lord, Thy words shall be my light
> Through death's vale and dreary night;
> Yea, they are my sword prevailing,
> And my cup of joy unfailing.